BARLEY WINE

BARLEY WINE

History, Brewing Techniques, Recipes

FAL ALLEN AND DICK CANTWELL

CLASSIC BEER STYLE SERIES no. 11

 A BREWERS PUBLICATIONS BOOK
Boulder, Colorado

Brewers Publications, Division of the Association of Brewers
PO Box 1679, Boulder, CO 80306-1679
(303) 447-0816; Fax (303) 447-2825

Printed in the United States of America
10 9 8 7 6 5 4 3 2 1

ISBN 0-937381-59-4

Please direct all inquiries to the above address.

Library of Congress Cataloging-in-Publication Data
Allen, Fal.
        Barley wine : history, brewing techniques, recipes / Fal Allen and
Dick Cantwell.
            p.   cm.—(Classic beer style series ; 11)
        Includes bibliographical references (p.   -   ) and index.
        ISBN 0-937381-59-4 (acid-free paper)
        1. Beer. 2. Brewing. I. Cantwell, Dick. II. Title.
III. Series
TP577.A38   1998
641.2'3—dc21   97-47343
                                                           CIP

To our families:

Barbara, Suzy, Patrick, and James Allen
Lucy and Nap Cantwell

Contents

Acknowledgments, ix

Introduction, 1

Chapter 1   The History of Barley Wine, 9
Big Beers: The Beginnings of Barley Wine
Barley Wine vs. Other Big Beers
Advances of History, Technology, and Procedure Define Barley Wines
Marketing Releases a Beer Called "Barley Wine," Tries Its Best, and Then Gives Up
The Americans Take Notice
Divergent Paths Keep a Venerable Style Alive

Chapter 2   The Flavor Profile of Barley Wine, 31
Barley Wines: What Is the Law?
Alcohol
Color and Clarity
Hops
Age
Yeast and Other Influences
Conditioning and Carbonation
"Families" of Barley Wines
Other Beers Defying
Classification

Chapter 3   The Five Elements: Malt, Hops, Yeast, Water, and Time, 53
The Malt Bill
Hops
Yeast
Water
Aging
Packaged Beer
Wood

Chapter 4   The Brewing Process, 81

Milling
The Brew House
The Boil
Pitching the Yeast
Knock Out (Casting Back) and Cooling the Wort
Fermentation
Cold Aging
Filtration
Packaging: Kegs vs. Bottles
Laying Down the Beer (Cellaring)

Chapter 5   Professional Barley Wine Breweries, 111

Chapter 6   Recipes, 131

Appendix A   Festivals, 145

Appendix B   Troubleshooting, 150

Appendix C   U.S. and Canadian Barley Wine Breweries, 157

Appendix D   Unit Conversion Chart, 164

Glossary, 166

Further Reading, 187

Bibliography, 188

Index, 189

About the Authors, 197

Acknowledgments

There have been many people who have contributed along the way. We would like to thank the following people in particular: Teresa Beddoe, Steve Bradt, Ray Daniels, Mark Dorber, Charles Finkel, Diana Lay, the Elysian Brewing Company, Toby Malina, Greg Noonan, Garrett Oliver, the Pike Brewing Company, Nick Redmon, Fiona Wood, all the brewers who sent us recipes and information, and Rick Buchanan and Phil Rogers.

Introduction

Back when we worked together, at what was then called the Pike Place Brewery, the day we brewed our barley wine was always a special occasion. Even though it was early fall, we would play Christmas music as we brewed, in allusion to the fact that the beer would not be released until the holiday season was in full swing. It was the only day of the year that we used the lightly peated Scottish distiller's malt from Crisp Malting in England in place of our usual Marris-Otter, invariably heaping it above the rim of our tiny mash tun and unleashing a smoky redolence that gave the normally rich smells of brewing a whiskeyish note. There was also something less tangible in the air. From the first mash-in until the last tipping of the hop back to get the final precious quart or two of wort, there was a sense of extra vigilance throughout the brewery as each of us made absolutely certain that we got the most out of every stage in the brew. It was a day of personal sacrifice, as buses were missed and phone calls made, in order that runoff and boil times could be extended in the pursuit of our desired massive starting gravity. And once the beer was in fermentation, each of us would check it daily, nervously monitoring the incremental drops in gravity as we tasted it for signs of greatness.

Because of the extra care taken in their crafting, as well as the extra amounts both of raw materials used and alcohol produced in the course of fermentation, barley wines are beers to make one sit up and take notice. They are beers that both brewers and consumers take seriously, and which require serious attention to detail. But lest it seem that we mean to intimidate, let us be clear that they can be made by mortals of limited means and resources, and made well. We ought to know—the brewing system on which in those days we brewed Old Bawdy, the Pike Place barley wine, was small, overworked, and cobbled together, but we had excellent raw materials, a wonderful yeast, and a great spirit of cooperation.

To the uninitiated, the very name "barley wine" seems calculated to confuse. A wine made from barley? Well, sort of. Few of the ales dubbed barley wines are truly in the range of alcoholic content of even sprightly wines, but that is the idea in naming them so. A classic British barley wine was the strongest ale brewed by whatever brewery saw fit to produce one. Often they were produced in connection with noteworthy events such as coronations or the births of royal heirs—fitting for ales brewed to starting gravities frequently in excess of 1.100. (By comparison, today the standard British bitter beers typically have starting gravities of 1.035 to 1.040, and industrially produced American lagers have starting gravities (SG) of 1.040 to 1.050.)

The alcoholic strength of barley wines can run as high as 14% alcohol by volume (ABV). It is true that in modern Britain, owing to a system of taxation based on alcohol content, the strength and durability of many beers calling themselves barley wines have slipped somewhat from the standards established a hundred or so years ago. In America, the supposedly consumer-protective decree handed down by the Bureau of Alcohol, Tobacco, and Firearms specifies that such beers must be designated "barley wine-style ales," a distinction that seems to cheapen and diminish the product in question (not unlike requiring distinguished imported beers of more than middling strength be labeled malt liquors).

In some cases barley wines were brewed only rarely, often commemorating a noteworthy event. These labels celebrated the coronation of Queen Elizabeth II and her twenty-fifth anniversary as Queen of England.

The centuries-old traditions of European farmhouse brewing used the parti-gyle system, where the first, second, and sometimes third runnings were boiled

and brewed separately. The heaviest first runnings of the mash were diverted to the richest (and headiest) of a diminishing succession of brews. Barley wines moved through brewing history somewhat confusingly yoked to other high-gravity or "big" beers, all typically in the range of 1.090 or more starting gravity and in excess of 8.5% ABV. They were beers to be laid down, like wine, in which the developing and melding flavors would show themselves to best advantage over time. In addition to alcohol and heightened hop flavor, the influence of bacteria and wild yeast could often be marked, especially as storage and maturation in wood was standard. Because of elevated starting gravities and an incomplete understanding of the performance and alcohol tolerance of yeast, they were also frequently sweet, with large amounts of residual sugar.

As an independent style, barley wine made its emergence early in the twentieth century. As commercial forces and trends saw fit to appeal to customers in a more organized and pervasive manner than simple word of mouth, the name "barley wine" began to appear with greater regularity in print. It was also at this point that most barley wines began to be produced from a single brew rather than as one of a series, as they had been in the past using the partigyle system. As such they came to be particularly prized, individual creations conceived and executed as something distinctive and rare, for which premium prices were paid. These beers were stored then served for some special occasion, holiday, or circumstance. Barley wines are now mainly identified with the winter holidays and are frequently grouped with so-called winter ales. American craftbrewers often release them at or in anticipation of Christmastime, a luxurious gift to customers who have been loyal throughout the year. At least this was the way we at Pike Place Brewery treated the unveiling of Old Bawdy. There were precious few quarter-barrel kegs to go around, and we always salted away a case or two with which to addle visiting brewers throughout the year.

Jealousy and hoarding are not generally exemplary qualities, but considering the care and effort that went into producing a yearly scant six barrels or so, the brewers at the old Pike Place Brewery can perhaps be excused for the reluctance with which our barley wine was disbursed. With the brewing of that beer we taxed our equipment, our yeast, our patience (and that of those waiting for us to turn up for dinner), our knowledge and experience of the brewing process, and our self-control as we gave it as much time as we could stand. Barley wines are brews that inspire ridiculous amounts of coddling and arduous care. Every procedural stage that can be undertaken, it stands to this kind of reasoning, can be stretched to the point of glorious over-performance, as it has been in the cases of other breweries of which we have heard: dry hops left in contact with the beer for more than a year; extract fortification to the point of not being fermentable; hand-bottled cases of laboriously painted bottles packed aboard ships bound for Japan. What is it about these beers that inspires such behavior? The answer lies in excess. With barley wine the demand can always be perceived as to add, to do, to wait more than with any other beer, indeed more even than the last time one brewed barley wine. As brewers we have always felt that for every privation laid at the feet of this one very special brew we would be rewarded by the result.

These days barley wine brewing is alive and well, if somewhat besieged in its native Britain. Its history is not continuous or easy to trace. Studying barley wine is like following footprints which disappear and reappear, forking and veering, stamping for a time in a circle and then dispersing, leaving trails that seem to go cold and then suddenly present a host of destinations. It's an enterprise requiring a few leaps of courage and fancy simply to consider the widely variant examples and information that is part of the same theoretically coherent style. We will challenge and define the parameters of barley wine, examining every stage of the brewing process to wring the utmost from ingredients, equipment, and procedures. We will explore the contributions of each of brewing's basic raw materials, including one not ordinarily considered—time. We will also offer practical hints based on our own home and professional brewing experience.

CHAPTER 1

The History of Barley Wine

Big Beers: The Beginnings of Barley Wine

In the traditions of British farmhouse brewing, dating back to the time of the Vikings, the beers similar to what we call a barley wine were brewed from the first mash runnings of a succession of beers, tapering in strength to ales light enough to serve children. Records are scant, of course, and where records are lacking rumor abounds, to the extent that even these smaller-gravity beers are reputed to have weighed in at gravities intimidatingly high. And the simple fact that hydrometers and exacting temperature regulation (innovations which took hold in the nineteenth century) had not yet come into general use during these largely undocumented times can only make the stuff of legend that much more elusive and glorious.

What could the really "big beers" have been like, then? Ponderous and bursting with the felling power of alcohol, bittered with armloads of hops, boiled for days, fermented for months, conditioned for years. Or so legend would have us believe. Research does not necessarily yield information less hyperbolic. Accounts by brewers are replete with exclamation points and phenomenal readings, once readings were taken, exalting these beers and setting them apart from the brews of daily commerce. Big beers they were, to read the ledgers and logs fortunately still available to us, necessarily brewed in smaller quantities and at great expense—anathema to the modern bean-counter—yet enjoyed in ever-increasing (and production-busting) volumes, until the taxman and changing tastes brought them, at least in the British Isles, virtually to their knees.

But then came the American microbrewery revolution. Of course, many of the seeds for this revolution were sown in the homebrewing and real ale campaigns of England. Devoted to rediscovering, emulating, and seeking to go one better than the classic beer styles of Europe and the British Isles, basement brewmasters and fledgling small-scale commercial brewers expanded their repertoires beyond "something pale," "something amber," and "something dark" to include the biggest beers their systems could produce. These high-gravity beers, usually released at Yuletide, were often as vaguely defined and as subjectively documented as their Georgian and Victorian counterparts.

Time, fortunately, has brought about scrutiny and scholarship on both sides of the Atlantic. Although continued commercial pressures in Britain have relegated all but a few examples of the style to production history, a golden age (tolerating deep copper and even russet examples) of barley wine brewing now reigns in America. Brewers here overdo it from summer to fall, producing beers bigger, maltier, hoppier and more alcoholic than anything existing in fact or history. These are the beers with which brewers exhibit their chops, their mastery of extract and isomerization, of patience and technique.

Barley Wine vs. Other Big Beers

For centuries brewing was a fairly inexact pursuit, its processes governed by empirical knowledge and example more than by the gauges and instruments we use today. It was simply known, for example, that the surface of water would become glassy when heated to a certain degree, which was suitable to raise the temperature of a mash. Equipment was rudimentary compared to today, baskets and other strainers performing the function of a lauter tun and its false bottom, a simple spigot affixed toward the bottom of the vessel constituting the single draw-off point. Fermenters were open and made of wood. Water quality was inconsistent, and beer was brewed and consumed at least partly because of its anti-pathogenic quality:

you could drink a mug of beer and not become ill, whereas most water carried no such assurance. Brewing was also a pursuit for cooler weather, largely because it was simply too difficult to avoid spoilage caused by heat, bacteria, and insects during the summer. Beer spoilage was always of great concern; beers of lesser weight and alcohol could not be counted on to hold, and so were consumed quickly. Beers of greater gravity and alcohol remained good for several months or a year. Often these beers of different weight were brewed from the same

 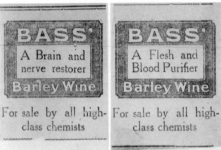

mash, the heavier beers from the richer first runnings, the lightweight, or table, beers from what was subsequently run off to the kettle. Much later, into the sixteenth and seventeenth centuries, once hops came into general use for their flavoring and preservative effects, they were used liberally to balance the flavor of these high-gravity beers.

There have always been big beers, produced in various ways and to various descriptions. Reference is made in the mid-eighteenth century to "malt wines" and "malt liquors" intended to compete commercially and in terms of strength and character with grape wines. Various healthful advantages of the strongest beers were also touted by those within the brewing industry relative to the effects of liquors and wines produced from other fermentable and distillable sources. Since the term "barley wine" was not widely used until the early twentieth century, other designations—such as "old," "strong," and "stock" ale—were often used. Not all of these beers would qualify as barley wines by today's standards, but they were the biggest and strongest beers produced by these breweries, and therefore can justifiably be considered the precursors of the style. Furthermore, since some of these designations have survived in variously interpreted efforts by both British and American brewers throughout the intervening decades and centuries, they provide both historical antecedent and ongoing comparative reference.

In addition to being generically referred to as "strong" ales, these beers were often called "old" simply because they were kept for a long time before being consumed. This was desirable because of the gradual melding and improvement of the flavors over time. Another term in common use was "stock ale," since the beer, as it matured, was considered a provision, or stock. These ales were frequently used for blending, lending character and complexity to more ordinary beers. Sometimes they were simply thinned out later to produce more of a lesser beer, thereby prefiguring the high-gravity brewing procedure widely employed by today's macrobrewers.

Because of the widespread use of unlined wood in both fermentation and storage, these big beers were commonly affected by the flavors imparted by resident microflora. In their book *The American Handy Book of Brewing*, authors Wahl and Henius chronicle analyses of many nineteenth-century beers, listing among their properties not only starting gravity and alcohol content, but a quantified lactic acid component as well (Wahl and Henius 1908). While these are all ways of plotting the flavor and character of a given beer, the lactic acid percentages of these big beers were sometimes strikingly high (1896 Bass No. 1 contained 0.288%, and a ninety-year-old Worthington Burton ale stood proud at 0.6095%), taking them out of the realm of nearly anything with which we are familiar today, and imparting a sour, or "vinous," character.

Conventional modern brewers, of course, are on guard against even traces of such influence. Though the terms "strong" and "old" continue to be appended to the names of high-gravity British and American ales, the name "stock ale" has all but exclusively emigrated to America, where in the nineteenth century it marked beers of greater strength and flavor. However, few big beers were brewed in America until fairly recently, and the term "stock ale" was an indicator merely of relative strength, and not of unparalleled power. These days it lives on only as a meaningless, vaguely venerable-sounding term to decorate beer labels and clutter classification.

Geography also came into play in the dubbing of the barley wine style. "Burton" ales were known as beers of rare strength, a fact based largely on the reputations of Bass No. 1 Burton ale and other similar beers from Burton-on-Trent. Burton ale is probably the clearest antecedent for barley wine as a distinct style. The numerical designation belonged first to Bass alone, the No. 1 being the biggest in a pantheon of sturdy beers produced there. More often a brewery's strong beers were emblazoned with multiple Ks and Xs, the greater number for greater strength.

The Durden Park Beer Club of London has conducted extensive research and experimentation on the production not only of the strong ales of British brewing history, but of once-prized porters, stouts, and more ordinary ales. Using archives and other research tools, they have collected sufficient

information to provide homebrew recipes in their book, *Old British Beers and How to Make Them*. Among their resuscitations are several big beers, including Truman XXK March Keeping Ale (1832) and various others amassing up to four Xs. This is as close as we will ever get to tasting the big beers once brewed by such nineteenth-century brewers as Bentley's and Tomson and Wotton.

Advances of History, Technology, and Procedure Define Barley Wines

The British precursors to barley wine were brewed in no particular locality, though it could be argued, largely because of Bass's foundation there, that Burton-on-Trent produced the big beers most closely allied with the modern definition of the style. Burton ales of the mid-nineteenth century were relatively pale beers, brewed with pale and amber malt, yielding starting gravities so high as to make the pulses of brewers race. The sugars associated with their typically high terminal gravities, however, could only perpetuate an elevated heart rate and eventual toothlessness on the part of immoderate consumers.

By the time Burton ales and strong ales came to be called barley wines (and brewed within the parameters emerging for the newly named style), the efficiency and general cost-effectiveness of pale malt was common knowledge, and it made up the bulk of the malt bill in more modern big beers. The sweetness of some of these beers, attenuated to percentages barely cresting fifty, as opposed to typical percentages of seventy or more in properly executed craftbrewed beer, can only have appealed to the collective palate of an earlier age. Several examples are cited by G. S. Amsinck in *Practical Brewings: A Series of Fifty Brewings*, with one beginning at 1.122 and finishing at 1.063 SG (Amsinck 1868). It is possible that the sweetness of all that residual sugar was mitigated by the sourness born of lactic acid. Not all strong ales finished at gravities this high, but there does seem to have been a tradeoff: In order to achieve massively high (above 1.100 SG) starting gravities, concessions would generally have to made when the yeasts used reached their limit of alcohol tolerance, gave up the ghost, and staggered to the bottoms of fermentation vessels. Yeast, for that matter, was only then becoming understood. Strong ales were also brewed in London at the time, but while attenuation seems to have been more thorough on the part of southern *Saccharomyces*, hopping rates were low enough that the resulting beers would still have been sufficiently sweet to strike a familiar chord within visiting Burtonites.

One reason for the astonishing starting gravities of the big beers of yesteryear had to do with the early brewing technique of parti-gyle, where a single mash produced multiple beers of descending weight and alcohol. Also, the technique of sparging, where water is systematically introduced over the surface of the mash in order to rinse out more entrenched sugars, had not yet come into general use. Parti-gyle goes a great distance toward explaining why the brewing of big beers was so commonplace, and how the product lines of the commercial breweries of earlier times came to be defined. In his excellent text *Belgian Ale*, Pierre Rajotte documents the brewing of a hierarchy of beers common throughout the brewing world (Rajotte 1992). There still exist breweries—such as Fuller's of London—where today the parti-gyle system is employed with great success.

Modern advancements aid not just in the production of the biggest beers, but in the control of all brewing where efficiency and consistency of gravity is a concern. Mash and lauter tuns are more efficiently designed and fabricated, and the methods of firing and the general configurations of kettles have improved. Coke and coal have given way to gas and steam. Swept kettles, in which a central paddle or agitator runs throughout the boil, can increase the vigor of the boil and hence the rate of evaporation. Other boil-augmenting designs include colandria, where the wort is forced by convection through a sort of super-heated tunnel fixed either inside or outside the kettle, and asymmetrical jacketing configurations which enhance kettle convection.

More is also known about raw brewing materials and how to wrest from them essences, extract, efficiency, and economy. Increased understanding of the enzymatic components of malt and the balance of malt modification for the production of specific beers makes brewing beers big and small more predictable, especially when such commonplace equipment as thermometers and hydrometers are used. Hop cultivation and analysis has come a long way since hops came into general use in the fifteenth and sixteenth centuries. Yeast technology has developed specific varieties suitable for the brewing of big beers as well as techniques for the effective propagation and enhanced performance of yeasts. Some would say that the generally more predictable result of modern brewing has come at a price—the sour flavor of yesterday's strong ales, for example, has been all but eradicated by modern technique. Still, it is now more possible than before to achieve a desired and reliable result.

Marketing Releases a Beer Called "Barley Wine," Tries Its Best, and Then Gives Up

In the second half of the nineteenth century, the Burton brewers Bass, Ratcliff & Gretton had a firmer grasp than most on the importance of easy product identification and a defined product line intelligible to the consumer. The familiar red triangle came into general use in 1854 as an identifying mark for the brewery's pale ale, and in 1866 a numbering system was devised to be used in conjunction with the more generic names by which the products were known. The lower the number, the bigger and stronger the beer, with No. 1 leading the way. A typical starting gravity for the No. 1 in 1890 was in the neighborhood of 1.110, with No. 2, another barley wine, fairly hot on its heels at 1.097. No. 3, Bass's old ale, weighed in at 1.084, and on down the list through mild and so-called family ales, the latter still beers of some substance (at least in the high 1.050s).

A separate hierarchy of numbers prefaced by the letter P denoted the dark beers of Bass, topping out with the P1, or Imperial Stout (1.098), and tapering on down to the P6 porter (1.060). In 1876 the red triangle became Britain's first registered trademark, followed by the red diamond, devoted to the ponderous and venerable No. 1, and the brown diamond, which emblazoned the dark beers.

Because of the numbering system, and the fact that through all the mergers and takeovers of the twentieth century it remains one of the world's strongest brewing brands, Bass is probably the easiest to track in historical terms. In all but continuous production from 1854 until its demise in 1995 (excluding only the years 1944 to 1954, when wartime rationing and postwar reconstruction determined the patterns of much more than the brewing of beer), No. 1 was first officially referred to as a barley wine in 1903. While the beer the brewery produced most of was its pale ale, referred to in logs not by a number but by the carefully penned triangle from its label, No. 1 was considered sufficiently viable commercially to warrant the brewing of a 200-barrel double batch approximately weekly as late as 1968. During this time, the very numerical designation became familiar enough to consumers for other brewers such as Tennent's to identify their barley wines as No. 1, frequently in conjunction with various other trade names. Tennent's claims credit for the first pale barley wine (as opposed to the darker, more traditional versions) in 1951. It may have been paler than No. 1, but the break from a darker tradition had already been made by the time their Gold Label came on the scene. Dark and pale barley wines were common in Britain through much of the twentieth century, but the combination of wartime malt rationing and the British systems of taxation based on starting gravity and alcoholic strength brought harder times to the production of really big beers.

Forced into an increasingly rarefied niche, barley wines underwent some interesting, mainly self-destructive, permutations. This resulted in marketing campaigns bullishly concentrated on alcoholic strength and a group of beers, some still knocking about England, billing themselves as barley wines but standing the hydrometer in the hardly Homeric 1.050s and 60s. "Strong as a Double Scotch—Less than Half the Price" blared advertisements for Tennent's Gold Label in the 1970s, seeming to appeal to the hammerheaded heavy drinker on a budget.

Emulating the famed Bass numerical designation, many breweries used "No. 1" when naming their beers, making it nearly synonymous with the barley wine style.

Marketing hyperbole would have us believe that barley wines command a substantial market share, but in fact demand has decreased in the

United Kingdom to the extent that, aside from a couple of heavyweight national brands, the brewing of barley wines has declined to the occasional, the commemorative, and the novel. Through all the adversity of rationing and taxation, through the attempts to glorify by advertising various other products taking a run at number one, Bass only once, for the ten year period between 1944 and 1955, interrupted production of its barley wine until the decision came to discontinue it in 1995. The Bass ads were dignified and amusing—"The proper beverage for this weather," suggested one. Another merely mimicked the ace of diamonds, the brand name No. 1 taking the place of the A.

In 1968 the Eldridge Pope Brewery in Dorchester, England, began producing Thomas Hardy Ale in commemoration of the fortieth anniversary of the author's death. Brewed entirely of pale malt to a gravity of approximately 1.125, the beer is aged for six months after fermentation and is vintage dated. The label, graced with a quote from Hardy's *The Trumpet Major*, boasts that the beer will age effectively for twenty-five years or more. At about 12% alcohol by volume, the beer was ranked by the *Guinness Book of Records* the strongest beer on earth in 1973, though in subsequent years the distinction has variously passed into other hands. The Hardy Ale, with its vinous flavors and russet hues, conjures to many the qualities of a classic old ale, but in name it is usually reckoned a barley wine. All this despite the fact that it is brewed with a lager yeast at ale fermentation temperatures. These days it is this beer that keeps its down-at-heel parent brewery afloat financially, its facility renamed the Thomas Hardy Brewery (in order, we suppose, to avoid the slightest confusion), which sadly devotes much of its energies to producing and packaging alcoholic fruit drinks.

In 1995, with production levels at approximately 1,200 barrels annually, Bass discontinued brewing its No. 1 barley wine. Not long before, in a shrewd bit of public relations pigeonholing, Whitbread, owners of Tennent's, moved exclusive production of Gold Label back to Sheffield, the site of the Exchange Brewery in which it had first been crafted. Clearly the market force of the style was on the wane. Notable producers of big beers in Britain continue to be Fuller's, which produces Golden Pride; Gale's, with its Prize Old Ale; and Young's, with Old Nick.

For the most part barley wine production has passed into the hands of small brewers. Offers have even been tendered to Bass by a particular small producer to contract brew the No.1, in order that it not be allowed to pass entirely from national—and world—consciousness.

The Americans Take Notice

Whether brewed by colonists making the best of a varied and inconsistent supply of raw materials or by later microbrewers doing much the same with perhaps even less knowledge and culture, the New World brewing of big beer began in both these embryonic phases with a certain amount of improvisation. In colonial times, an inconsistent supply of malted barley resulted in fermented beverages called beer but employing high percentages of sugar, molasses, and other indigenous fermentables such as corn, and often flavored with materials at hand like sassafras and pine. The parti-gyle system was commonplace. In 1667, for example, a refectory brewery at Harvard University allotted various amounts of small and strong beer for hierarchical consumption by students, faculty, and administration.

Ale in general came under attack when large numbers of German and central European brewers immigrated in the second half of the nineteenth century, bringing their culture of lager brewing into prominence. The beers brewed in early America didn't measure up in terms of weight or alcohol to British brews. There is little documentation, in fact, of the brewing of strong ales in America, other than commemorative examples such as Ballantine's storied Burton Ale, issued at Christmastime as late as the 1950s and reputed to age well for twenty years or more.

The first American microbrews were not beers to be laid down. They were brewed on makeshift concatenations of dairy equipment, hardware store tubing, and institutional soup tureens, combining a poor selection of raw materials with knowledge gained from a couple of well-thumbed British brewing manuals. Many beers of the movement's early days were notable mainly for the stand they took against the insipid standards set by the nation's industrial brews. With much room for improvement in both the facility by the brewers and the equipment and materials available to the small-scale producer, a big beer produced by the average early American microbrewer would almost certainly not have aged well. But as knowledge spread and more high-quality beers were produced, it became inevitable that the fledgling brewers would work to produce big beers.

In 1975 San Francisco's Anchor Brewing released Old Foghorn, a pale, sweet barley wine of a reputed 1.100 starting gravity. Bottled in six-ounce "nips" and occasionally kegged for draft sales, the beer became prized by microbrew connoisseurs, even turning up outside official distribution networks. Within several years Sierra Nevada Brewing in Chico, California, offered Bigfoot, a fiercely hoppy barley wine which varies slightly in color year to year. The Bigfoot is also prized, and only limited quantities are allowed outside of California. These two remain the preeminent American barley wines in terms of style and, for all their vagaries, market availability. The late 1980s and early 1990s have witnessed a wave of barley wine brewing, in which the style has become almost *de rigeur* in the trotting out of accomplishments on the part of small brewers. Barley wine ranks as one of the more popular entries at the Great American Beer Festival in Denver, Colorado, the nation's biggest and most competitive beer event. Brewpubs are most likely to brew them, since the extra expense of a single legendary batch is more easily justifiable than it might be in a larger and more accounting-driven production setting. It could be argued that barley wine (along with India pale ale) is a style these days kept alive by American brewers.

It makes sense that barley wine would appeal to Americans. These are beers with swagger, where expense and time are readily sacrificed in the interest of producing the best, the biggest, the strongest of beers. They are beers with bragging rights, overstated in both malt and hop character, pampered, coddled, cajoled, then released amid fanfare.

Divergent Paths Keep a Venerable Style Alive

Within the boundaries set by the production of extremely high-gravity beers, there exists a lively dialogue on their effective balance and execution. Brewers across Britain and the United States can be generally characterized geographically in terms of their preferences, with a balance toward hoppiness increasing as one goes westward, first across the Atlantic and then into the Pacific Northwest. The English bent is toward maltiness and maturity, with age playing perhaps more a part in the perception of a "finished" flavor. It is uncommon for a British barley wine to be very bitter, though some examples show a pronounced hop character, particularly when drunk young. East Coast brewers are perhaps more aggressive in terms of hopping rates than England or the midwestern and southeastern states, but cannot match the more heedless northwestern barley wines. Even California examples trail the bitterest barley wines of their Oregon and Washington colleagues and neighbors (Rogue Brewing's Old Crustacean and Pike Brewing's Old Bawdy spring to mind). It is difficult, and entirely subjective, to say which of these interpretations is the truest, but disagreements like these can only further the interest and culture of a venerable, and much disputed, beer style.

Parti-Gyle Experiment

Simply out of curiosity, we ran an experiment using the parti-gyle system, mashing 21 pounds of malt to a medium-thin consistency with an unmeasured amount of water at 150 °F (66 °C), running off without sparging, and adding liquor again to yield a smaller beer. Four and a half gallons of wort with a starting gravity of 1.084 were first collected, followed by 5 gallons of 1.038 wort. Naturally the specific results would vary with vessel size and configuration, as well as with experience, but the practical point is made that once first runnings are taken, other beers can yet be made from a single mash. Hair of the Dog Brewing in Portland, Oregon, has also employed this method, taking second runnings from their legendary Adam beer (1.094) and producing a "small" beer of 1.050 starting gravity. Their name for it? Small beer.

CHAPTER 2

The Flavor Profile of Barley Wine

Barley Wines: What Is the Law?

Barley wine is undoubtedly a style given to excess. In terms of the raw ingredients used, the limits to which equipment is taxed during the brewing process, and the resulting gravities and levels of alcohol evident in the finished product, there is no other style as full of itself. It therefore isn't surprising to find a certain amount of disagreement as to what constitutes a proper example. There are, in fact, a number of proper versions of the style, each with historical and geographical precedent, and each matching the original qualities. It should also be taken into account that, given the pride with which brewers regard these crowning beers of their achievement, a certain amount of hyperbole—and even falsehood—must be sorted through in the digestion and assimilation of all that information (and all that alcohol). It is certainly

possible to overdo a style that beckons to the coura-
geous. Many among us, in fact, are well aware that
some finish impossibly sweet; that some are
overblown with hop bitterness and the aromatic,
often vegetal character of finishing hops; and that
some bear an alcoholic content way past mellow. No
disrespect is meant to brewers giving it their all in the
crafting of an ale calculated to administer the knockout punch. However, an even hand is a necessary
conceptual tool to apply in both the formulation of a
successful recipe and the proper and patient render-
ing of the brew.

Alcohol

Just as the nineteenth- and twentieth-century Burton and London versions of strong ale and barley
wine varied in taste, British and American types of
barley wine need to be distinctly defined and credited
for their various flavor interpretations. The British are
placed at something of a disadvantage owing to a tax
system which fiscally punishes producers of stronger
beers. The Free Mash Tun Act of 1880 began the taxation of beer based on starting gravity and the resulting alcohol content. The situation was worsened by
the rationing and increased taxes during and following the world wars. The result is that in many cases
today beers not sufficiently big and strong, historically, are being called barley wines. We remember a

conversation with an accomplished British brewer, given to the crafting of iconoclastic and excellent beers from a small facility in Yorkshire, who boasted that yes, indeed, he made a barley wine—of 1.057 starting gravity. Well, a fine beer it may have been, but at such a gravity it simply cannot be considered a barley wine. Other English examples bear names like Old Headcracker, implying a heedless strength sufficient to X the eyes, but all too often the appellation is wishful and relative, calculated mainly to rise above the best bitters of pedestrian—even driving—potency.

Simply put, barley wine is the biggest beer you can brew. To say that something less demanding deserves to be in the company of ales for which the appropriate trouble was taken is to diminish the style entirely. There are, to be sure, a number of beers brewed in the British Isles that do rise to the heights required of barley wines deserving of the name, and we pay them homage. We feel strongly that for a beer to be termed a barley wine, a starting gravity of at least 1.080 should be achieved, with no less than 8.5% ABV. Even setting the levels this low is fairly liberal. Consider Bass No. 1, to many ways of thinking the barley wine of record, which bore (until its demise in 1995) a starting gravity in excess of 1.100.

Other examples include Lee's Harvest Ale from Manchester, Gale's Prize Old Ale from Horndean, and, though its flavor complexity seems to have suffered over the years, Tennant's Gold Label. Some would maintain that beer styles, like language, change with the times, and for some styles this may reasonably hold true. But barley wine is the biggest, most excessive of the ales and should not be diminished by marketers or brewers admitting anemic beers to such a rarefied category.

Color and Clarity

Parameters of strength and alcoholic content having been expressed, there are only a few other requirements for barley wines. To differentiate barley wines from darker old ales and heady imperial stouts in the same range of alcohol, the style suggests that while a barley wine does not necessarily need to be pale, it should not be opaque. Held to the light, it may be dim or russet, even burnt in color, but it must be seen through. It should consist of all barley malt, or barley malt with sugars and malt syrups employed to augment gravity and perhaps impart, or diminish, color. Sugars and other syrups, of course, bring their own qualities to a brew and must be judged and used with a knowledge of their effect. But they have their purpose, especially for the small-scale brewer concerned with the limitations of equipment.

Cane, corn, or even uncomplicated malt sugar can, when used in excess, deprive the finished product of the complexity that separates a true barley wine from a mere exercise in octane. The use of other grains or adjuncts can only muddle presentation. A faintly persistent fashion among American West Coast brewers over the past several years has been to introduce wheat as a major fermentable material. These "wheat wines" have not necessarily claimed to be barley wines (and we have tasted excellent beers crafted under this rubric), but it should be clear that inclusion of wheat or oats or spice spins formulation and execution of barley wines off into a possibly delicious, but separate, world.

Given the age at which most barley wines are intended to be drunk, clarity is an issue that should mainly take care of itself. Over time, even unfiltered, unfined, or otherwise unclarified beer is likely to settle out nearly as bright as if these treatments were employed. In the case of stubbornly unflocculent yeast, however, measures may need to be taken (see chapter 4). Absolute clarity is not something to be insisted upon, but care should be taken in the serving and dispensing of long-aged beers so as not to disturb the sediment, or lees, so the beer can show itself best.

Hops

With hops, balance is the key, of course. A roaringly hoppy barley wine which teeters atop a spindle of malt character is no more appropriate to the style than a lubricious syrup of prodigious starting (and finishing) gravity. American, British, New Zealand, or Australian hop varieties seem most appropriate to the style, but we see no reason that an accent of German or Czech character would set a barley wine beyond subjective limits. Aroma hops can be heady and hearty, or they can be barely there.

Age

Many barley wines are crafted with the idea that by the time they are consumed, a hop character perceived in the young beer as aggressive will have diminished to a fine balance. This is part of the trick, of course. Familiarity with the bittering hop used and its diminution over time is one of the marks of the accomplished brewer of barley wine, or any aged beer. Other metamorphic qualities, such as the continued degradation of slow-fermenting sugars and the breakdown of unstable material in the malt component, must be taken into account. But the gradual marrying of the mercurial hop and the stolid barley-corn is a key to the brewer's art.

It isn't an absolute rule, of course, but it does seem that a beer of this size can best be appreciated with *at least* ninety days of aging. Given the vagaries of packaging, especially where home- and small-scale craft-brewers are concerned, a longer aging period is not necessarily better, but with proper packaging control having been achieved (i.e., the minimization of oxygen, appropriate bottle and keg head space, and the reasonable stability of the product at packaging), most barley wines will show improvement over at least a couple of years.

It is no accident that pale barley wines of sufficient stability to withstand (and benefit from) the effects of age were increasingly produced in the early twentieth century. The modern perfection of procedures and increased understanding of the scientific processes involved have made it possible to produce pale beers able to stand up to the aging periods previously associated with the darker "big" beers. One reason for the stability of these darker beers is the forgiving nature of the melanoidin component in dark malts. As George Fix writes in *Principles of Brewing Science*, "Because dark malts are rich in melanoidins, some dark beers have extraordinary flavor stability" (Fix 1989). This explains historically why the darker big beers were able to stand up to time, and serves to set apart the specifically designated "old" ales of modern times from the paler barley wines.

Yeast and Other Influences

One might think that the selection of a yeast for producing a barley wine would be a fairly obvious thing. Flavor characteristics, of course, should first be considered. Next, attenuation and alcohol tolerance must be taken into account as the most important mechanical factors. Various tricks are often employed, however, in order to achieve or circumvent the practical considerations (and limitations) inherent in the choice of a particular yeast. A yeast, in short, can be inspired to the task by such treatment as repeated rousing during fermentation and the agitation of the casks in which it has been packaged. An ale yeast able to perform well in all of these areas is the best choice, but often breweries, or homebrewers, make the easy choice and employ either lager or champagne yeasts. These are known to perpetuate the purposeful churn of attenuation, often at the expense of body or ester production essential to the appreciation of a big beer. The choice must therefore be carefully made. Your everyday ale yeast may do the job, and it may not. It is often simply a matter of experimentation to discover this, since in many cases the limits of a particular yeast cannot be known unless they are challenged.

While consistent house flavor can be considered a matter of honor in the production of a family of beers, if the ale yeast to which you are accustomed will not do the job alone, then certainly look elsewhere for something able to perform sufficiently to produce a creditable barley wine. A good place to start might be procuring the same yeast used to produce a high-gravity beer that you like, either through the advice of colleagues or the staff of either a homebrew shop or a yeast lab. Should you run into trouble with attenuation, lager or wine yeasts may be just the ticket to completing a moribund fermentation. However, because of other qualities they can impart—notes of sulfur or over-attenuated "thinness," as well as over-carbonation through continued cold fermentation—they should not be the primary fermenting agent, and should largely be considered steps of desperation.

Some bacterial activity and/or wild yeast (particularly *Brettanomyces* and *Lactobacillus*) may be evident in some barley wines, especially if they have spent time in wood (this was particularly true of the big beers of yore), but this elusive note is not to be insisted upon and is only to be pursued by the intrepid brewer. Even the professional brewers best known for these flavors in their beer do not fully understand the workings of their bacterial cohabitants—they simply are. The world (as well as your regional yeast bank or neighborhood homebrewing supply) contains ale yeasts ready, willing, and able to produce barley wines of note. Find one and let it do what it will.

Conditioning and Carbonation

Condition, or the amount of carbonation evident in the finished beer, is something often ignored where barley wines are concerned, mainly because allowances are often granted beers "of a certain age." A barley wine of character should not be dismissed simply because it has ceased to dance with a level of effervescence commonly associated with more sprightly and mass-produced beers. It should not, however, be completely dead. Yet this is quite often the case with old casked barley wine—effervescence has been sacrificed for the mellowness, the viscosity, the sugary display.

Allowances can be made, but for reasons associated with long-term conditioning, barley wine is a style that responds well to in-package secondary conditioning. Both cask and bottle conditioning provide the means for an awakening of condition, and the limited yeast activity associated with the process should consume any oxygen present, thereby guarding against stale off-flavors. Extra trouble is involved in the priming of ales which have long lain dormant. Often a measured quantity of active yeast cells must be introduced along with the priming sugar or gyle. But it certainly can be worth it; to render each individual bottle a self-contained atmospheric entity is a labor worthy of these largest of beers. The amount of priming used, of course, is critical in order that the bottles and casks in question may be poured, and not spew energetically out. Some of the best barley wines we have tasted have combined the fruit, the age, and the hop and malt balance, with a gentle yet lively degree of condition. It is not to be demanded, but it can be a particular pleasure.

Defining Barley Wines

The 1985 Campaign for Real Ale (CAMRA) Dictionary of Beer, by Brian Glover, defines barley wine as:

A strong, rich, and sweetish ale, usually over 1.060 OG [original gravity], dark in colour, with high condition and a high hop rate. Extended fermentation times render most barley wines potent in alcohol: for this reason, and because of their heavy palate, they are usually sold in "nip" bottles containing one-third of a pint. Whitbread's Gold Label is probably the most common example.

And from the 1997 Great American Beer Festival "Guidelines to Beer Styles and Medal Categories":

Barley wines range from tawny copper to dark brown in color and have a full body and high residual malty sweetness. Complexity of alcohol and fruity-ester characters are often high and counterbalanced by the perception of low to assertive bitterness and extraordinary alcohol content. Hop aroma and flavor may be minimal to very high. Diacetyl should be very low. A caramel and vinous aroma and flavor are part of the character.

Original Gravity (°Plato): 1.090–1.120 (22.5–30.0)
Apparent Extract/Final Gravity (°Plato): 1.024–1.032 (6–8)
Alcohol by Weight (Volume): 6.7–9.6% (8.4–12%)
Bitterness (IBU): 50–100
Color SRM (EBC): 14–22 (28–44)

"Families" of Barley Wines

Recognizing that barley wine exists in a number of interconnected streams, the characteristics of the more prominent of these should be chronicled.

The Trent, the Thames, and Others: English Barley Wine Brewing

It's compelling to consider Bass No. 1 the strand that at its ultimate unraveling, in 1995, left the British barley wine scene generally somewhat unbound. Having stood for so long, through a combination of quality, longevity, and corporate soundness, as the example often emulated (and always mentioned), its presence—and absence—resonates throughout the British culture of barley wine brewing. Indeed, in a Campaign for Real Ale (CAMRA) tasting of barley wines and winter beers as recent as late 1996, Bass No. 1 (as brewed, as it is occasionally, on the small museum system at Bass) took top honors over many other more generally available examples. And having made, in our estimation, the clearest break from the tradition of darker big beers, it occupies a defining space where the development of modern barley wines is concerned.

Bass No. 1's relative paleness, its single (or sometimes double but never

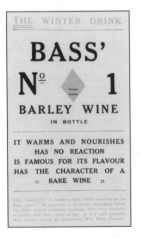

THE WINTER DRINK

BASS' N⁰ 1
BARLEY WINE
IN BOTTLE

IT WARMS AND NOURISHES
HAS NO REACTION
IS FAMOUS FOR ITS FLAVOUR
HAS THE CHARACTER OF A
:: RARE WINE ::

parti-gyle) brewing procedure, and its aromatic and flavor staying power reminiscent of the enduring glow of cognac, maintains a group of standards to which other British brewers of the style must pay

attention, if not outright homage. Which isn't to say that other successful and wonderful barley wines must conform in every way. There are darker barley wines which burn and calm, which send a pleasing display of flavors and aromatic esters across the senses of the drinker. There are ones produced by the parti-gyle system which represent a venerable and service-able part of tradition. Fuller's Golden Pride is one of these, less potent runnings resulting in the smaller, but delicious London Pride and Chiswick Bitter.

Mellowness, or a certain softness of flavor, is a watchword for the British version of the style these days, with toasted sugar or caramel arising from either an extended boil or being actually employed as fermentables; the moderate presence of alcohol; and an array of fruity esters including but by no means limited to apricot, cherry, coconut, pineapple, and dried banana. Generally these are not terribly bitter beers, and especially not once typically aged. Hop aroma will similarly diminish with time.

The effects of age, in fact, are the benchmarks of British barley wines. It is not uncommon to detect the characteristics of slight oxidation, though given heightened alcohol and elevated hop levels, this is not necessarily a pejorative. A certain amount of air is essential for the enjoyment of barley wine, as the flavors and effects uncurl from long confinement. We have tasted leaky kegs of barley wine that have admitted air for months before discovery, and been amazed at the beer's resilience. Barley wine is not invulnerable while aging, but it is more able than most to fend off the attack, and even to incorporate this adversary as an interesting flavor element.

To a point, the same is true of bacterial infiltration. Some of the world's most notable beers are brewed in some of the world's dirtiest breweries, but there exists a difference between a comfortable and traditional background of native microflora and simply not taking the trouble to keep things clean. The fact of this paradox should be a marvel, not an excuse for shoddy brew house cleanliness. Naturally, the introduction of oxygen and bacteria are to be guarded against, but with the realities attendant on age and imperfect packaging, the best should be made of an unanticipated situation that may have become interesting.

The Northeastern United States—The Great Between

One doesn't hear the term mid-Atlantic much anymore, and almost never on the American side of the water. It has been used to describe accents and tendencies calculated to appeal to both English and Americans as at once familiar and somehow, unthreateningly, foreign. Taking elements from each system of expression, the mid-Atlantic idiom and pronunciation is especially identified with news reporters and disc jockeys whose voices are heard around the world. Well, the northeastern American way of making barley wine could be considered a sort of mid-Atlantic version of the style whose poles exist in Britain and along the northwestern coast of the United States. It carries most elements of the British approach—age, mellowness, a usually less-than-robust rate of hop bittering—but, free of the punishing British tax restraints on the production of big beers, it is given to producing barley wines of a size commensurate with the biggest of the West Coast examples. Here and there about the region as well, hops are used with abandon—this is America, after all.

While barley wine in the United States started in California, this style in the Northeast claimed a more direct

Third Coast Old Ale

Kalamazoo Brewing Company's Third Coast Old Ale rates up there in gravity, easily big enough to be a barley wine.

Three different labels used for George Gale's Prize Old Ale, a beer deemed a barley wine by its brewer.

relation to old ale. This may have something to do with marketing and the labeling requirements that "barley wine" must be qualified with "-style ale," a cumbersome appellation less romantic and evocative than "old." A great many barley wines from all quarters, of course, bear the word "old" as part of their name whether they have been aged or not, a bit of brewer's license as responsive to folksiness and tradition as to history. Just the same, it seems that somehow age began as a firmer prerequisite to northeastern big beer brewing than in other parts of the United States. We remember seeing casks of aged "Winter Warmer," a barley wine of low effervescence and belly-warming alcohol, sitting atop bars in the Northeast ten and more years ago, when most often West Coast breweries were releasing their seasonal big beers with three months or less of aging. While many of these beers qualify as barley wines (and often are considered so by their brewers), they are frequently dubbed old ales. This is interestingly true at Gale's of Horndean as well, where though the beer is named

Prize Old Ale, the current brewmaster considers it a barley wine.

We have remarked a certain muddiness of interpretation where the line between barley wine and old ale is drawn, explained away by the notion that the term *old ale* is really only generic, referring to the maintenance of an old style, like the German term *altbier*. Old ale as a style may be elusive and misunderstood, but it is named so because of the aging of the beer, and not because of historical uncertainty. This confusion is by no means limited to the East Coast of the United States, but as its biggest and most excessive beers are often named and designated old ales, some discussion of the question is warranted.

Another fact about not just eastern barley wine brewing but craftbrewing in general is that the first brewpubs on the East Coast were started by Englishmen, and were therefore philosophically more responsive to familiar precedent than to the New World standards being set in the wilder and less stylistically respectful West. Readier availability of English cooperage, equipment, and expertise also came into play. This fact, combined with the relative youth of the craftbrewing revolution on the East Coast, would dictate a generally more conservative approach to classic brewing styles.

There are exceptions, however, and as brewers continue to migrate and the movement ages, distinctions blur. Already there are brewers out of regional character providing contrast to consumers eager to become involved in friendly controversy. National and regional beer festivals also provide arenas for comparison, and help keep alive the dialogue that leads both to disagreement and compromise. This is not to imply there is an eastward-creeping manifest destiny of bitterness and aroma, but history does dictate that things will balance.

Northwestern Barley Wines

As Bass No. 1 must be designated the definer of an emergent style in England, Anchor Brewing's Old Foghorn, from San Francisco, must first be considered when discussing American barley wines. Initially brewed in 1975, it was the earliest barley wine of the craftbrewing movement in America, the one that started all the fuss about big beers here. In its flavor profile, however—pale, malty, but with enough hops to constitute sufficient excess of lupulin—it is to be deemed more a barley wine of the world than a specifically Northwest example of the style.

The Bigfoot of Sierra Nevada, first brewed some years after Old Foghorn first sounded, undoubtedly leaves a bigger imprint on the development of a style peculiar to this geographical quadrant. Every bit as big as Old Foghorn, Bigfoot is less sweet and more completely attenuated, resulting in an increased presence of alcohol and a cleaner palate-effect. This allows its prodigious hop display a reign loved by its adherents and decried by those demanding a more classical balance. It is generally the favorite of brewers in the Northwest, though as one ranges south into California a more marked appreciation for age and lesser attenuation fuels lively discussion around both the pub and the judging tables.

As the barley wine style has spread to other noteworthy breweries of the Northwest, it is most often a similarly fierce hop attack that heads up the list of priorities in the crafting of barley wine. Most of the barley wines produced here are aged; some of them are pronouncedly sweet (BridgePort's Old Knucklehead comes to mind); they are all big in starting gravity, in the range of the mid-1.090s or more; and they are often on the pale side and aggressively hopped. They are, simply put, the most excessive of a style given to excess.

There are a couple of simple reasons why barley wines in the Pacific Northwest are so very hoppy. One is the proximity of one of the world's great hop-growing regions. Another is that Seattle and Portland,

two of the region's most prominent brewing centers, both have extremely soft water, allowing the introduction of prodigious amounts of hops without the excessively vegetal astringency that would result in brewing waters of greater mineral content.

Other Beers Defying Classification

There exist a number of other styles of big beer which, though not necessarily claiming to be barley wines, should probably be considered from that perspective as an exercise in definition. The first of these is imperial stout. These ales were brewed in the British Isles, we have all been told, for importation to the Russian Imperial court, where they were enjoyed by czars and such other historic luminaries as Catherine the Great. Certainly big enough to be historically considered a dark barley wine (as does beer expert Michael Jackson), imperial stout has lately been forced to wander an inhospitable landscape of classification. It has over the years been shuttled from category to category in the judging at the Great American Beer Festival (GABF), finally coming to roost in its own separate category. Indeed, in *Stout*, Michael Lewis considers imperial stout such a break from traditional stout styles that he devotes to it only a brief discussion (Lewis 1995). As the GABF has recognized, it is in fact its own style. Any broader category into which it fits would have to be a fairly generic one devoted to all strong ales, including barley wine.

Like barley wine, imperial stout is a style all but vanished in England (Samuel Smith's and Courage providing notable exception). Revived and reinterpreted in America, its best-known practitioners include Bert Grant of Yakima Brewing and Malting, Garrett Oliver of Brooklyn Brewing, and John Maier of Rogue Brewing. Grant prescribes that along with complexity, depth of flavor, and an elevated alcoholic strength, an imperial stout must be opaque, the latter guideline suiting us fine in setting it apart from its barley wine cousin. Bass's P2 Imperial Stout once headed up that brewery's roster of dark beers, and we have tasted it recently at the Bass Museum Brewery's pub.

There are a few Belgian beers which lie outside the designations afforded that beer-rich country's many hefty zymurgic offerings, and that, if sneaked into a barley wine tasting, might stand proud, stylistically speaking. Bush beer in particular, from the Dubuisson Brewery in Leuze, bears a character quite in keeping with British barley wines. At a starting gravity of 1.096 and an alcoholic content of 12% ABV, as well as with its brightness and flavors of caramel and toasted sugar, it belongs more among the English big beers for sale a ferry ride away than in the company of the ponderous beers of its homeland.

Another good example is Stille Nacht, from De Dolle Brouwers in Esen. It is a beer which, despite the decidedly Belgian character of its yeast-related flavor profile, ages very much in keeping with barley wines.

Holland as well (De Hemel Brewery in Nijmegen, for example) produces beers in this realm.

Probably a further stretch are the enormous lagers of Germany and Switzerland, most notably Hürlimann's Samichlaus from Zürich and a couple of examples from Kulmbach, EKU 28 and Kulmbacher Reichelbräu's Eisbock. Since they are lagers, and bear the typical, if enhanced, flavor and style characteristics of that realm of brewing, few would suggest that they should be considered barley wines. Thomas Hardy Ale, on the other hand, is brewed with a lager yeast, albeit at fermentation temperatures conventionally connected with ales, and while it might be considered irresponsible to categorize it a lager, is it much  different to suggest assessment of these Germanic big beers as belonging to the same camp? Samichlaus and EKU 28 are simply monsters by any stripe of interpretation, often vying for world's strongest beer honors (Thomas Hardy is frequently a combatant as well), but the clarity of their yeast character combined with the bright, syrupy nature of their flavor makes them something decidedly other than the big ales of Britain and America. The process of producing *eisbock*—prescribing light freezing and the subsequent, alcohol-favoring removal of ice—would in its own right remove it from contention, but as one of the world's biggest beers it bears mention.

CHAPTER 3

The Five Elements: Malt, Hops, Yeast, Water, and Time

Professional brewers and homebrewers alike have spent innumerable hours in cross-table discussion on the subject of which ingredients produce the best and most proper flavors in a particular style of beer. The purist will claim that, in order to create an appropriate flavor profile for a particular style, you must obtain the raw materials from the region in which that style originated. Another might counter with established examples that break the rule, such as a traditional Scotch ale made with a Belgian yeast, a quintessential German Pilsener made with New Zealand hops, or an award-winning barley wine made with American malt. The discussion goes on and on. There can be no conclusive answer. There is no doubt that certain raw materials yield distinct flavors and aromas. The question is, what flavors do you want to design into your beer and what raw materials and processes should you use to achieve those flavors?

The Malt Bill

Barley wines feature malt character. Even the hoppier barley wines will have big broad malt shoulders from which many other flavors will hang. To make a beer of such fortitude it is necessary to use two to four times the normal amount of malt per gallon of beer. With that much grain going into a brew there is no way around the fact that you are going to get plenty of malt flavor. The type of malts you choose (the specialty malts as well as the pale malt) will have a dramatic effect on the final flavor of your beer. We have found that for barley wines, the behemoths of the beer world, a less complex grain bill is often better.

Pale Malt

Pale malt is the backbone of any beer, and this is especially true of barley wines. Pale malt is the main source of fermentables, and fermentables are what making a barley wine is all about. The sheer quantity of pale malt in a barley wine causes it to stand out as the major contributor to the flavor profile, thus the choice of pale malt will greatly influence the flavor of the final product. The pale malt that you use should be highly modified, thereby converting easily and generating the most fermentable sugars possible. English or American two-row malt works best. American and continental six-row malts should be avoided.

English pale ale malt is the best choice for this style of beer. It is highly modified and low in protein and has a more complex flavor than American malts, which are generally malted to macrobrewery specifications. This complexity of flavor is due in part to a more prevalent tradition of hand-craftsmanship (i.e., floor malting) among the maltsters of the British Isles. British malt flavor is rounder and has greater depth of character with an almost bready or biscuity flavor. Marris Otter pale malt is the best of the best in this arena, much favored and sought after by independent British brewers and brewers of traditional cask ales.

This is not to say that you cannot brew a good barley wine with American malt—you most certainly can. Sierra Nevada's Bigfoot is an obvious example. That said, it should be noted that American pale malt will be lighter, less complex, crisper, and "cleaner" in flavor. Beers brewed with American barley, that is grown and malted to Anheuser-Busch's and Miller's specifications, will naturally have a different flavor than that of beers brewed with malt designed and produced to make more flavorful beers. Therefore you must decide what kind of malt flavors you want in your barley wine and then choose a pale malt accordingly.

Specialty Malts

When deciding on specialty malts always remember to keep it simple. Too much, or too many types, of specialty malt will cloud the flavors of your beer and make them muddled and indistinct. A more even hand is required in the use of these malts in the brewing of big and aged beers. Keep in mind that the extended boil and conditioning times associated with the brewing of barley wines will magnify the effects of a proportion of specialty malt which in a smaller beer seems just the thing. Too much specialty malt can also leave too many complex or unfermentable sugars in the finished product. This can make the beer cloyingly sweet, as well as unstable over time.

Extended boiling times will increase the malty sweetness

found in the beer through caramelization of the sugars. In *Scotch Ale*, Gregory Noonan reports that caramelized wort sugars give a beer a more malty flavor than the use of crystal malts, and that these caramelized sugars are a major component of a Scotch ale's rich caramel flavor (Noonan 1993). Scotch ales are also generally associated with high terminal gravities and residual sweetness, qualities that in a barley wine are difficult to avoid even under the most judicious of circumstances. Carmelization of the wort during boiling also produces an increase in color through nonenzymatic browning reaction. The longer you boil, the more caramelization of sugars and the greater the formation of melanoidins, or color components, and thus the darker your beer will become. It has been estimated that as a result of these reactions you can get as much as 25% of the total color of an all pale malt beer during a ninety-minute boil. For these reasons we suggest that no more than 15% of your total grain bill be colored or specialty malts.

Our research shows that most professional breweries go very easy on the specialty malts in brewing their barley wines. They go even easier on the dark malts, if they use them at all. A little bit will go a long way. The use of dark malt should be kept below 2% of the total grain bill.

When choosing specialty malts, go with just one or two carefully selected styles. Crystal malt, used sparingly, adds color, sweetness, and body to your beer. It will give it an orange to reddish glow. Munich and dextrin malts will give your beer some nice malt flavors and add a small amount of additional color. In moderation, these malts can work well with less complex (i.e., American) pale malt, giving the beer a nice grain flavor. In general, keep in mind that notes and subtle accents of malt difference can give drinkers and critics much to talk about in the appreciation of your barley wine; an overly commanding specialty malt presence may make them want to put it on their pancakes.

Adjuncts

Some brewers will add sugar or malt extract to the kettle to achieve higher gravities. We recommend keeping this practice to a minimum. If using malt extract, keep it to 40% or less of your total fermentables. In homebrewing keep it to 60% or less. That way it will have little or no effect on the flavor of the beer. If you use non-malt sugars like corn, cane, beet, or rice, we recommend keeping them to 15% or less of your total fermentables. These sugars will provide fermentables without adding much of their own flavor. At these percentage levels, the use of adjunct sugars and extracts should not have a significant impact on the overall taste of your beer. Some of the non-malt sugars do have interesting flavors that can work well in beer, as evidenced by their long-standing use in British brewing. Just remember to use them sparingly and with a certain purpose in mind, such as increasing gravity or providing an interesting additional flavor. Do not let them thin or overpower your beer.

Hops

We remember reading somewhere that you cannot put too much hops into a barley wine—words almost certainly written by someone from the U.S. West Coast where the word *hops* is almost synonymous with beer. But after tasting some of our early efforts at homebrewed barley wine, we feel sure that whoever wrote that statement was incorrect. Just the same, you can add an enormous amount of hops and still make a well-balanced and enjoyable beer. The international bitterness units (IBU) in barley wines usually run in the range of 50 to 90, and there are some commercially available examples that even exceed 100. These latter examples have high terminal gravities and residual sweetness, which helps balance all that hop bitterness.

Like many other areas of brewing, there are two distinct camps concerning the use of hops in barley wines—hop flavor and bitterness versus malt flavor and sweetness, crisp hoppiness versus malty sweetness, West Coast versus East Coast. Whichever camp you fall into, the challenge is to make a balanced beer, achieving the bitterness that will be appropriate for the style of barley wine you want to create. And as with malt, the hop that you choose will have a dramatic effect on the flavor profile of your beer. This holds true for the bittering hops as well as the flavor and aroma hops.

When choosing hops, in addition to looking at flavor and hopping rates, there are a couple of other things to be aware of. First, a high-gravity brew will have lower efficiency of hop utilization than a lower-gravity brew. Also, the components that produce hop aroma and flavor are the first things to go as a beer ages. Iso-alpha-acid, the bittering component, also decreases with age. As far as overall flavor is concerned, we have observed that highly hopped beers tend to age better than less hopped beers for the first two to four years. After this time the less hopped beers, perhaps initially balanced to be less dependent on hop character, seem to fare better as the highly hopped beers begin to swing out of balance.

Boiling Hops

Research (our own and that of other brewers and scientists) shows that boiled hops not only provide bitterness but also contribute significantly to hop flavor. The degree and type of flavor contribution is variety specific. Some hops, such as Chinook, will contribute a very strong and discernible flavor while the effects of other varieties will not be nearly as pronounced. Another important variable is that some hop varieties produce a harsher bitterness than others. It

Hop Chart

Hop varieties vary from year to year as well as from one growing region to another. This chart is for the crop grown in the year 1996. Information provided by Morris Hanbury and John I. Haas.

Hop Variety	Alpha Acid%	Beta Acid%	Cohumulone (% of Alpha Acid)
Ahtanum	4.5%	5.5%	32%
B.C. Kent Golding	5.0%	2.3%	23%
Brewer's Gold	9.0%	4.8%	35%
Bullion	9.0%	4.6%	32%
Cascade	6.0%	6.0%	37%
Centennial	11.0%	4.3%	30%
Challenger	7.5%	3.0%	22%
Chelan	13.3%	9.5%	35%
Chinook	12.0%	3.5%	32%
Cluster	7.0%	5.0%	39%
Eroica	12.1%	4.5%	35%
First Gold	7.5%	3.5%	33%
Fuggle	4.5%	2.8%	26%
Galena	12.0%	3.5%	32%
Golding	5.5%	2.4%	23%
Hallertau	5.6%	4.2%	28%
Herald	12.0%	5.2%	37%
Hersbrucker	4.0%	5.0%	23%
Liberty	4.8%	34.0%	27%
Magnum	14.0%	4.5%	25%
Mt. Hood	5.0%	5.0%	23%
North Down	8.0%	5.3%	29%
Northern Brewer	8.0%	3.6%	29%
Nugget	12.8%	4.5%	27%
Perle	7.0%	3.9%	29%
Phoenix	10.4%	4.8%	30%
Saaz	3.5%	4.0%	26%
Spaltz	8.3%	5.8%	26%
Styrian Golding	5.0%	2.5%	28%
Symphony	16.5%	5.2%	44%
Target	11.2%	5.1%	35%
Tettnang	4.0%	3.6%	25%
Tillicum	13.3%	9.5%	35%
Ultra	2.5%	4.2%	26%
Willamette	5.9%	3.8%	32%

has been suggested that this harsher bitterness is related to a higher cohumulone level in the hops. Hops with high alpha acid contents often (but not always) have a high level of cohumulone. Despite this, we prefer using higher alpha acid hops for bittering when brewing a barley wine, something in the range of 8 to 16%. And although high alpha hops may contribute slightly to harsh bitterness, they have the very real advantage of reducing wort losses in the kettle due to hop absorption. A brewer would use only half as many Galena hops (14% alpha acid) as compared to Northern Brewer hops (7% alpha acid) to achieve the same bittering in a beer. Less hops used means less wort absorbed by the hops and thus left behind in the brew kettle at the end of the boil. Using a high alpha acid hop will also allow you to avoid some of the vegetable flavor you may pick up from boiling an enormous hop mass of low alpha acid hops. Another benefit to lessening the amount of hop material is that it will reduce the likelihood of clogging your heat exchanger. One of the varieties that breaks the general rule of high alpha acid hops is Magnum. It is in the 15 to 16% alpha acid range, yet has a very low cohumulone level and a soft bitterness.

Finishing Hops

Your choice of finishing hops will depend on the style of barley wine you want to make. Are you trying to brew a traditional English barley wine or one of those newfangled American jobs? Do you want a beer that has American, British, or perhaps German hop flavors? Do you want loads of hop flavor up front or should it be part of the subtle background character? There are no hard and fast rules. If you are planning on the traditional route, you need to use British hops like East Kent Golding, Fuggle, Challenger, or Northdown. If you prefer an American flavor, you might try Liberty, Centennial, Columbus, Chinook, or Cascade. Some people look at the beta acid levels to give them an idea of how much flavor component that particular hop variety will give.

Yeast

If malt is the backbone of a barley wine, then yeast is its soul. Many say, in fact, that the choice of yeast and all it brings to the flavor of the finished beer is the most important choice a brewer makes in the formulation of a recipe. For those of you who desire a less philosophical definition, Gregory Noonan, in *New Brewing Lager Beer*, writes: "Yeast are a nonphotosynthetic, relatively sophisticated, living, unicellular fungi, considerably larger than bacteria. Brewer's yeast are of the genus *Saccharomyces*" (Noonan 1996). Whatever the malt and hop components, yeast is responsible for the majority of the "beer" flavor that we taste. Changing the yeast strain can completely alter a beer whose raw materials were otherwise unchanged.

Yeast Flavor

The first thing to consider when selecting a yeast strain is its flavor and ester production profile. If you like several of a brewery's beers, then their yeast strain (or one like it from Wyeast or other yeast suppliers) will be what you want to look at first. There are some commercial examples of barley wine made with bottom-fermenting yeast, but we feel that barley wines really should use a top-fermenting yeast. An ale yeast is much more likely to give you those heady and powerful flavors and aromas you are looking for. Even restricting your selection to ale yeast, you are still left with literally hundreds of choices.

Flavor and ester production are functions of fermentation temperature as well as yeast strain. Fermentation temperatures should be kept in the range of 66 to 72 °F (19 to 22 °C). This will help keep ester production down to a reasonable level while ensuring its character becomes part of the beer.

Again, if you enjoy other beers made from a particular yeast strain, then that yeast will probably work well for you in a barley wine, at least from a flavor perspective. Other variables also need to be considered when choosing a yeast strain, including alcohol tolerance, attenuation, and flocculation.

Alcohol Tolerance

Can the yeast you have chosen tolerate alcohol? Many yeasts can ferment beers of low- to mid-range alcohol content beautifully, but when called upon to ferment a big beer, run out of energy and quit with the job half-finished, leaving you with a high terminal gravity. This will not only make the beer too sweet, it also will leave unfermented simple sugars in the beer, thus creating an environment in which bacteria can easily bloom. This is an important consideration during extended aging periods.

In order to successfully process a barley wine wort, the chosen yeast strain will have to be able to take the beer to at least 8% ABV. Most ale yeast will be able to handle 8 to 9% ABV. Some yeast strains will go up to 12 to 14% ABV. The Pike Brewing Company's yeast has fermented beers to 12.5% ABV and might have gone higher had there been any more simple sugar to consume. So, if you plan on making a truly Herculean brew, you may have to call your local yeast supplier to find an appropriately ambitious yeast strain, or borrow some from a friend.

It should be mentioned that some brewers use more than one strain of yeast to ferment their beer—

one for flavor that will do the early part of fermentation and then another strain (added later) to take over and finish up the fermentation. The first yeast pitched (added to the cool wort) is generally an ale yeast. It is allowed to ferment normally, and when it begins to flag, a second more alcohol-tolerant yeast is pitched, taking the beer into the homestretch of attenuation. Some home and professional brewers use champagne yeast for this second pitching because of its alcohol tolerance. Other brewers will pitch a more alcohol-tolerant ale yeast or a lager yeast to continue attenuation even during cold conditioning. We prefer to stay with a beer yeast—an ale yeast in particular—because a champagne yeast often creates non-beer flavors. Its attenuative properties also come at a price because champagne yeast (as well as lager yeast) can digest more of the complex sugars that might best be left in the finished beer for flavor and mouthfeel.

Attenuation

Attenuation is a measure of the amount of sugar in the wort that has been converted by the yeast to ethanol and carbon dioxide. Some yeast strains can only utilize the simple sugars found in wort, the single- and double-chain sugars glucose, fructose, sucrose, and maltose. These yeast are called low attenuators or unattenuative yeast. Other strains can metabolize three-chain sugars like maltotriose and other trisaccharides. These strains are categorized as medium to highly attenuative yeast strains. Still others, called super-attenuative strains, can break down and use four-chain sugars like maltotetraose.

The yeast strain you use should have a relatively high level of attenuation so that it metabolizes all the one- and two-chain sugars and most (or all) of the three-chain sugars. This will make a beer that is less likely to be overly sweet as well as leaving less "available" sugars in the beer that bacteria may consume in later storage. A good rule of thumb is that your final gravity should be 20 to 28% of your original gravity. Be certain that the yeast you choose is both a good attenuator as well as alcohol tolerant, since it won't matter how attenuative the yeast is if higher levels of alcohol shut down metabolic functions and cause it to leave the fermentation unfinished.

Flocculation

Flocculation is a yeast's ability to clump together and fall (or rise) out of solution. When making barley wine, you don't want a yeast to drop out of solution before it has finished its job of fermentation. Many, but not all, of the yeast strains available to you will be strong flocculators, as this is a common characteristic of brewer's yeast. When using a yeast strain that flocculates well, it may become necessary to mechanically keep the yeast in suspension by "rousing" or stirring it. (This will be discussed in greater depth in chapter 4.) Generally, the more attenuative yeast strains are less flocculant.

With all this in mind our preference leans heavily toward a good strong British ale yeast (though our experience includes excellent results with American varieties). Maybe something borrowed from one of those nice London breweries.

Oxygen

Although not strictly an ingredient in beer, oxygen must be present in the cooled wort in order to bring about a vigorous and complete fermentation. This is an extremely important point and one often over-looked or underserved by many brewers. Contrary to concerns of over-oxygenation, the fact is you cannot put too much air, or oxygen, into the wort. At ale fermentation temperatures wort simply cannot hold enough dissolved oxygen to be a problem. On the other hand, should you fail to introduce enough oxygen at the outset, the yeast will have difficulty starting fermentation and will almost certainly not complete it. This will leave you with an unattenuated, sickly sweet beer. In addition, this will make the beer more susceptible to bacterial infection.

When we brew a barley wine, we aerate during the entire knockout (cooling) process, being careful to avoid foaming the wort out of the fermenter. We shoot for 10 to 14 ppm of oxygen in the wort as it enters the fermenter. This can be obtained by diffusing 1.5 liters per minute for the length of your knockout.

If you are using air (as opposed to oxygen) at ale fermentation temperatures, it will be more difficult to achieve these concentrations, since air is mostly nitrogen. We suggest that you diffuse air in at 3.0 liter per minute. Air should be sterile-filtered before being injected into the fermenter. For the best results, try to get the oxygen or air into solution in-line, on the way to the fermenter. That will give the gas the maximum amount of contact time and hence a better chance to dissolve into the liquid. In-line aeration can be increased by using a sintered metal "stone" (similar to those used for carbonating beer). This will produce a larger number of very fine bubbles, which in turn creates a greater amount of surface area and thus better absorption of gas into the wort.

Water

Although in barley wines water makes up, technically speaking, a smaller percentage of the beer's total composition than it does in other beers, it is still by far the largest proportional ingredient. Water plays a very important role in every aspect of the brewing process. The water you use for brewing and the minerals it contains will have a significant impact on the final flavor of your beer. If your water is potable (if it tastes good) you can brew with it. Just because your water is not the same as a specific classic brewing town or region does not mean that you won't be able to create a great beer. From a historical perspective, there really is no one classic region for barley wine brewing, or at least none more specific than England in general. High-gravity beers were (and still are) successfully brewed all over England in areas having very different water chemistry. The mineral contents in these various areas run the gamut—from London, where the water is relatively soft, to Bass in Burton-upon-Trent, which is known for its hard water.

Maximum Levels of Minerals for Suitable Brewing Water

Bicarbonate	< 50 ppm
Calcium	< 270 ppm
Calcium sulfate	< 800 ppm
Calcium chloride	< 100 ppm
Chloride	< 100 ppm
Copper	< 10 ppm
Iron	< 1.0 ppm
Maganese	< 0.2 ppm
Magnesium	< 100 ppm
Magnesium chloride	< 100 ppm
Magnesium sulfate	< 100 ppm
Nitrate	< 20 ppm
Nitrite	< 0.1 ppm
Phosphorus	< 10 ppm
Silicate	< 30 ppm
Sodium chloride	< 300 ppm
Sulfate	< 650 ppm
Zinc	< 0.6 ppm

Burton Water

There really is no "classic" brewing town for barley wine, but if there was, it would probably be Burton-upon-Trent. Both in the past and present, it remains a major brewing center, famous for hundreds of years for its pale beers.

It is the home of Bass Brewing, the makers of the "first" commercial barley wine, the Bass No. 1, whose production unfortunately ended in 1995. (There is no commercially made barley wine, that we know of, brewed in Burton today.) Many old brewing books have suggested using the same water for barley wines as for bitters or pale ales. So we include a brief overview of the Burton water supply.

Mineral	Amount in Burton Water
Sulfate	640 ppm
Calcium	270 ppm
Bicarbonate	200 ppm
Carbonate	140 ppm
Magnesium	60 ppm
Chloride	40 ppm
Sodium	30 ppm
Nitrate	30 ppm

All the general rules concerning water that apply to other beers apply to barley wine brewing as well, with the foremost guideline being to know what is in your water. You can obtain a full water analysis from your local water department at little or no cost. If your water comes from a private well, send it out to a local laboratory for analysis. Once you know what's in your water, you will have a better idea of how to treat it. High levels of iron, bicarbonate, particulates, or organic material should be avoided. The latter two

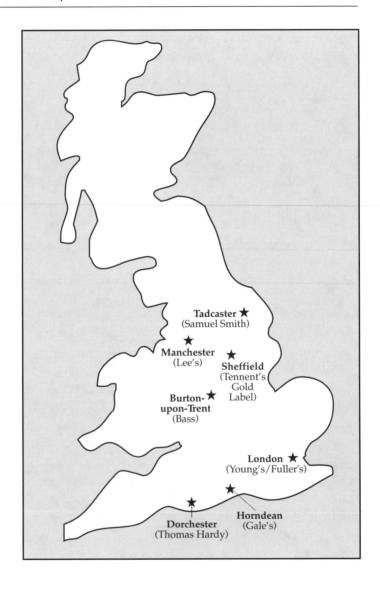

may easily be removed by filtration. Bicarbonate of over 50 ppm can be removed by pre-boiling your brewing water; iron should be less than 1 ppm.

For more information on water as it relates to beer, consult the reading list on page 187. These books cover the subject in great detail.

We think, if we are not mistaken, that we have now fulfilled our obligation to talk about water.

Aging

Time is the fifth ingredient in barley wines. This is true in all phases of barley wine production, beginning with an invariably extended brew day. Fermentation almost always takes longer with a high-gravity brew because two or more weeks may be needed for the beer to reach its terminal gravity. The beer may begin with an impressive surge only to reduce to a slow but steady pace in the second or third day. If this happens, don't panic. As we will discuss in the beginning of chapter 4, there are things you can do to help with fermentation. Once the initial fermentation is concluded, the warm (58 to 70 °F, 14 to 21 °C), or diacetyl, rest needs to take place. This rest, which tends to be longer for these larger beers, may take one to two weeks, and will allow the yeast the proper amount of time to reduce diacetyl and other metabolic by-products of fermentation. This is an important step in producing all beers, including lagers; but it is especially important for high-gravity beers, where there are greater amounts of diacetyl created during fermentation. Without this rest, the beer may have a pronounced "butterscotch" flavor or other taste defects.

After this rest, it is time to chill the beer. The most common cold-aging temperatures range from 34 to 40 °F (1 to 4 °C), but aging can also effectively be done at traditional cellar temperatures (50 to 55 °F, 10 to 13 °C). Some Anglophile ale producers may claim that so traditional a British beer style should be conditioned no colder than the norm of cellar conditions in its homeland. In the past, lacking the needed technology, cellar temperatures were as cool as they could practically get them. We feel cellaring temperature is a matter of choice. A benefit of cold-aging is that it precipitates out proteins that can cause haze. Haze can have a deleterious effect on the visual aspect of the beer as well as a significantly negative impact on the flavor of the finished beer. Colder temperatures will cause more of these proteins to bind together and precipitate out of suspension. Thus the colder (and longer) the aging period, the less of these undesirable elements will remain in the beer, and the cleaner and brighter the beer will both look and taste. It's difficult to justify the slavish attention to tradition when the benefits of improving upon it are (so to speak) so clear. Most brewers agree that high-gravity beers, like barley wines and old ales, require substantial additional aging. We like to give a barley wine a minimum of ninety days of cold storage prior to going into packaging.

Packaged Beer

Now the beer is ready to be packaged. After packaging, the beer will need to be aged for a minimum of seven to ninety more days. Providing proper care is taken in the course of filling the appropriate containers, the beer can improve in this post-packaging aging period for many years. This aging allows the flavors to meld and mellow. Hop bitterness will lose some of its edge, and hop aroma will fade. The changes can be many and varied. We have found that most barley wines improve with one to two years of post-packaging aging. Some will age well for six to eight years. A few can even go beyond ten years before negative effects are detected. There are even those that claim longevity of their barley wines into the next generation. As a rough rule of thumb, the higher the starting gravity, the more gracefully a barley wine will age.

As discussed, the hop component of an aged beer will break down first. The more highly hoppy barley wines tend to be better with one to three years of age. The less hoppy counterparts tend to age slower, doing better over the long haul. The temperature that a bottle (or keg) of beer is stored at is also important for the aging process. John Hansell (publisher of the *Malt*

Advocate) recommends aging packaged beer at cellar temperatures (50 to 60 °F, 10 to 16 °C). He has found that beers aged within this temperature range fare better than those aged at cooler or warmer temperatures. Aging at cellar temperature allows beer to continue to work and mature without accelerating decay. The beer will often be drier, fruitier, and softer while still retaining some hop notes. Our research confirms Hansell's findings. As with wines, more age is not always better. One must hope to catch a vintage bottle when it is at its peak. The trick is in proper storage and anticipation.

Barley wine does improve with age, so make sure to vintage date bottles and kegs. And remember to set a few bottles/cases/kegs aside for yourself. Over the coming years, you'll be able to go to the reserve stock, pull out the special vintage bottles, and share a taste with selected friends or visiting brewers.

Wood

Should beer be aged on wood in modern times? For centuries, beer was made and aged in wood vats and casks. There were few other materials of which brewing vessels of any size could be constructed. Indeed, wood contributes flavors of its own. It harbors both the flavors of earlier packaged (and conditioned beverages) and resident microflora, particularly lactic acid bacterias (like *Lactobacillus*)

and wild yeast (like *Brettanomyces*). All of these flavors, which are all but unknown in the modern brewery, have venerable antecedents.

There is endless debate as to how much "wood" flavor the beers of old would have had. Today, outside of Belgium, there are very few breweries using raw wood for beer storage of any length of time. Marstons in Burton and Firestone in California use raw wood for fermentation vessels, but the beer does not remain in them long. The wooden serving casks that you see in use today are nearly all lined with pitch, paraffin, or plastic, each of which removes any chance of flavor contribution from the wood.

There is a good reason these casks are lined— there is no way to completely sanitize wood. Unlined wood harbors bacteria and wild yeast that will dramatically change the beer. There is virtually no way to control or predict exactly what flavor will be produced. All but a few brave or eccentric breweries have abandoned the practice. The Gale's Brewery in Horndean near Portsmouth, England, still conditions its Prize Old Ale in wood—a fact which imparts a quality that is possibly closest to an old British beer than anything else available commercially today. It is truly a beer produced without apology or fear.

Eliminating the issue of wild flora and fauna within wood, the question still remains, should beer be aged in wood? We have used, with success, French limousin oak chips to add flavor to some of our higher-gravity beers. The use of wood chips is common in home and professional winemaking, having mainly to do with the economy of chips over costly imported barrels. Oak can give beer (or wine) a richness, a smooth vanilla tone, and a subtle woodiness. We found that only French oak was mild enough to use without overpowering, and even then it needed to be used sparingly—1/2 to 1 ounce per U.S. barrel.

A relatively new development in the world of beer aging is maturing in wood from other industries. This has been done in the Scotch industry for many years. Some American brewers now age their bigger beers in used whiskey, port, and other types of barrels. The few we have tasted (many are still aging) have been very exciting. The contact with these barrels subtly changes the beer and imbues it with some wonderful flavors. Greg Hall at the Goose Island Brewery in Chicago aged some of their imperial stout in Jim Beam barrels and it was awesome. The Pike Brewery has done similar experiments with very favorable results. The stout flavors seem to meld and blend very well with the leftover whiskey flavors soaked into the wood of the barrel. We are hopeful that more of this type of experimentation will continue.

CHAPTER 4

The Brewing Process

For the most part, the steps and the equipment employed in brewing barley wines are the same as those required for brewing other British ale styles. The difference lies in the technique used for each of the steps. Brewing a barley wine requires extra vigilance and extra attention; unless you make the commitment to brew nothing but barley wines and other big beers, and thereby devise systems and procedures that eventually settle into second nature, the brewing of these biggest of beers is likely to require extra work and craft. The whole brewing process must always be considered as one of continually making procedural decisions to adjust the enterprise along the way. The question to remember is how can you get that much more of everything out of your brewing system?

Milling

Time was, brewers were also maltsters, and needed to be concerned with every aspect of procedure connected with the processing of raw grains. Nowadays, of course, nearly all brewers receive their grain already malted, and while pre-delivery specifications and procedures need to be maintained, all that really has to be done to prepare for mashing is to crack or mill the malt.

The milling (cracking open) of the grain exposes the starch, or endosperm, which subsequently will be converted to sugar in the mashing process. This cracking or grinding of the malt is accomplished by means of a roller mill. Roller mills are adjustable to allow for the size variations inherent in different types of malt. Herein lies the rub: the husk of the grain must be cracked open without pulverizing the whole kernel. It is very important not to overcrush your malt. This is true with the brewing of any beer but especially true with barley wines. Barley wines, in fact, can use two to four times as much malt as an average brew, resulting in a greater bed depth in the lauter tun and thus much higher screen pressures. On a good day, a barley wine runoff can take fifteen to forty-five minutes longer than a usual brew, but an overly crushed malt will cause the mash bed to become compacted. It can gum up, slowing the proceedings to a trickle, and eventually stick your runoff completely, turning your brewing day into a living hell, or at least a major bummer. In addition, small chunks of husk can be sucked through the lauter screens, carried over to the kettle and, when boiled, result in unrefined grain flavors and harsh, astringent bitterness. All of these reasons make it very important to properly mill your malt.

If you are a professional brewer, control lies as close as the adjusting screw on your malt mill. But if you are a homebrewer at the mercy of the milling facilities of your local homebrew supply shop, try to make sure their mill is set properly to not overly crush the grain. If in doubt, ask to see a sample first. Sure, the shop person may think you're being a beer geek, but so what? They won't be the one dealing with a stuck runoff if the mill is set too tight.

The Brew House

The traditional British brew house has two main vessels: the combination mash/lauter tun and the kettle. In some cases it may also have a hop back (strainer) or, if a modern brewery, a designated whirlpool for the separation of hops and trub.

The Mash Tun

In many ways, the single-step infusion mash conducted in a mash/lauter tun is the best way to brew a barley wine. Because these systems are designed to be used with highly modified pale base malt, there is but one conversion temperature to achieve. That means no decocting, no continual mixing of the mash as you go from one temperature rest to the next, and no pumping of the mash from one vessel to another.

These procedures have their place in the crafting of certain beer styles or when using undermodified malts, but they can be counterproductive when brewing a barley wine. Each of these additional procedures not only reduces the mash to finer particles, but also beats a little bit more of the air out of the mash—air that helps buoy up the mash bed and keeps the mash bed from collapsing on itself and compacting. That little bit of air becomes even more important with larger amounts of malt in your mash tun.

The Monster Mash

If you are like most brewers, you probably brew a barley wine only once or twice a year, so when you do you want it to be special. You want it to last a long time, both in the bottle and in the memories of those who drink it. And you also want it to be a huge beer. A brewer's first inclination is to fill the mash tun to the very rim with as much grain as it can possibly hold. Resist this impulse. The deeper the mash bed, the slower the runoff, and the greater the chance of compacting or "setting" the mash. Setting the mash will reduce your runoff to a trickle, extend the runoff and

A traditional English mash tun insulated with wood staves.

sparge into a multiple-hour affair, and increase the likelihood of having to use desperate measures that may lower your gravity. Brewing barley wine will almost certainly tax your brewing system, as well as your patience and concentration, but even the pursuit of excess has its limits.

Instead of overfilling your mash tun, you may opt for sparging less (adding less water to rinse the grain bed of its sugars). This will give you less wort in the kettle, but the wort you collect will be of a higher gravity (i.e., have more fermentable sugars). Remember the ultimate goal: brewing the biggest beer the best you can. Lowering the yield is almost certainly preferable to overfilling the mash tun and its attendant compromises. It may mean doing multiple brews to fill a fermenter or settling for a lower yield, but the improved quality of the beer and the greater ease of brewing will be a fair trade-off. We therefore recommend that one try not to exceed two to three times normal mash bed depth. Mash consistency should be in the range of medium to medium thick, using slightly less than 1 quart of water (0.9 liters) for each pound of malt.

Even with the most effective mash program, you will not achieve 100% conversion of starch to fermentable sugars. Some percentage (approximately 30 to 35%) can be expected to remain as "unfermentables." Since there is an increased volume of malt in the mash tun, you will get a fairly large amount of unfermentable sugars in the wort. This is simply a fact. One thing to keep in mind is the optimal temperature/performance ranges for the two enzymes native to malted barley—alpha- and beta-amylase. To help keep unfermentables at a reasonable level, and hence to further the attenuation necessary in avoiding an overly sweet beer, shoot for a mash temperature on the medium-low side between 145 to 152 °F (63 to 67 °C), the span in which the two enzymes, alpha- and beta-amylase, work most effectively together. For the maximum percentage of fermentable sugars, the mash temperature should be maintained at 145 to 146 °F (63 °C) for sixty minutes or more. If the mash temperature is higher than 152 °F (67 °C), the wort will likely be overly sweet and dextrinous, resulting in a poorly attenuated and unbalanced beer. With the amount of malt being used, there will be plenty of unfermentables for sweetness, complexity, mouthfeel, and body. Another added benefit of a more completely converted mash is that it makes for an easier runoff.

Recirculation (Vorlauf)

As with the brewing of other beers, it is advisable to recirculate some of the first wort through the grain bed to remove grain husks and other particulate matter that has inevitably passed through the lauter plates, or screens. The easiest and most consistently effective way to do this is with a pump. If you don't have a pump, you can gently draw the wort from under the screens and gently pour it back on top of the grain bed. Be careful not to "drill" a hole into the mash bed when returning the wort to the top of the grain. Homebrewers can avoid drilling a hole in the mash by simply placing a plate on top of the surface of the grain in order to catch and diffuse the flow of returning wort.

Many professional breweries are fitted with diffusers or adjustable piping for this purpose, but even then some improvisation may be called for. We have seen this effectively done with a plastic snow shovel used to spread the return flow evenly over the mash bed. Recirculation must be done slowly so as not to collapse (or "set") the bed or disturb the sediment that has settled to the bottom of the vessel during the ninety-minute mash. Slowly recirculate until the wort begins to run clear or "bright." But beware: sometimes the wort won't get completely bright, and the brewer is faced with the temptation of continuing recirculation at the risk of setting and/or cooling the mash bed, thereby compromising ongoing runoff. You may have to settle for only removing the larger particles during the recirculation, and hope that things will clear up as the runoff proceeds. Once the clarity of your wort is satisfactory, begin running off to the kettle.

Runoff and the Sparge

Start the runoff slowly. It is inadvisable to "pull" too hard (runoff to quickly) as this may compact the mash bed. If the runoff is too fast, not only could the mash set, but you run the risk of not thoroughly extracting all sugars from the mash. With the volumes of grain demanded of brewing barley wine, runoff is likely to begin slowly in any case. Don't force it, be patient. If you are going to sparge start adding the 170 °F (77 °C) sparge water while the wort level is still about an inch above the grain bed. Do not wait until the bed is completely exposed. When the sparge is underway, the hot sparge water will heat the mash bed. Once the hot sparge water has rinsed out some of the sugars and helped to loosen the bed, then slowly speed up the runoff. Remember, it is very important not to start speeding up the runoff too soon. Don't let the grain bed get exposed but keep the depth of sparge water above the grain to less than two inches. An excess of water will increase the weight pressing on the grain bed, thereby posing the risk of compression, which in turn will reduce the runoff in both volume and efficiency.

If your mash bed does set (and it's happened to all of us), you can try to underlet. Underletting is the infusion of hot water into the mash tun *under* the false bottom or lauter plates, thus "lifting" the mash bed off the plates and decompressing the mash bed. This can be a lifesaver, but it can also be a compromising procedure, particularly for the brewing of big beers. Try to avoid long or repeated underletting, since, if done to excess, it can greatly reduce the gravity of your wort.

We have found it extremely useful to measure the gravity of the runnings (wort) when entering the kettle. This allows for tracking its progress and minimizing unpleasant surprises later on. By taking gravities periodically throughout the runoff, you get a good idea of the overall gravity in the kettle, and of how much sugar is likely to remain in the grain bed. A gravity reading is also a good indicator of when and how much to sparge and when to stop the runoff. When making a barley wine, our runnings typically start at 17 to 20 °Plato (1.068 to 1.080) and gradually go up into the mid- to low-20s (1.084 to 1.092). They then start to fall off towards 15 °Plato (1.060) or so. At that point, briefly sparge the grain bed. We usually stop the runoff when the runnings are between 12 °Plato (1.048) and 9 °Plato (1.036), depending on the kettle volume.

At the end of barley wine or other big beer runoffs, brewers with holding tanks or additional kettles will often continue to sparge and collect the lower-gravity runnings. They will use these last runnings to make a "small beer." The making of a second, or small, beer is a tradition that dates back to the earliest days of brewing and is a good, and enjoyable, way to utilize the fermentables that would otherwise go down the drain.

The Boil

The boiling of the wort, always an important aspect of brew house operation, becomes especially so in the brewing of barley wine. It is often not given due consideration by some home- and microbrewers (as well as by equipment manufacturers). Once the clear wort has been separated from the grain husks and residue through lautering (straining), it needs to be boiled. The wort now contains carbohydrates (fermentable sugars, unfermentable sugars, and starch), as well as protein, amino acids, and other yeast nutrients. Boiling the wort brings about several necessary and beneficial changes: sterilization; halting of enzymatic action; protein denaturing and coagulation; hop bitterness extraction and isomerization; color development; sugar caramelization; evaporation and wort concentration; and the driving off of some undesirable elements (like dimethyl sulfide).

Both the quantity (length) and the quality (vigor) of the boil are important. Without a strong rolling boil, many of the above reactions will not fully take place. Good brewing equipment is designed to facilitate the "turning" or rolling of the boil. Kettle design often incorporates a mechanism that facilitates wort rotation or agitation. Some of the more common devices are internal or external colandria, agitators, swept bottoms, or a kicker panel that delivers more heat to one side of the kettle than the other, thus causing the wort to turn or roll over. These mechanical advantages can also help reduce fobbing during the boil. A brewer should hope to achieve at least twelve complete turns or kettle rotations of the wort in an hour.

Stabilization

Stabilization of the beer is brought about by boiling in three ways: sterilization, the cessation of enzymatic activity through heat denaturing, and protein coagulation. During the boil, wort proteins react with other proteins, as well as with phenolic substances derived from malt and hops, to form large aggregate complexes that will precipitate out of solution. This precipitate is known as "hot break." The process of protein coagulation is not solely heat-dependent. It is favorably enhanced by the physical action of steam bubbles passing up through the wort. The albumin fractions of wort protein accumulate on the surface of the boil around the steam and air bubbles, causing higher localized concentrations that will more readily flocculate (aggregate) and precipitate. Because of this, and other reasons that relate to hop utilization, the boiling action in the kettle needs to be vigorous. Without a vigorous rolling boil, you will not properly coagulate and precipitate the proteins in the wort.

Physical stability is important for every style of beer but especially so for barley wines because they face such extended storage times. Insufficient protein coagulation and removal can cause problems in the fermenting and conditioning processes, as well as in the finished beer. These problems include incomplete fermentation, tannic/astringent or harsh bitterness, permanent chill or protein haze, and oxidation reactions such as beer staling and poor filtration. A proper and vigorous boil helps reduce all these problems.

Too long a boil, however, can have its own negative effects. It can cause the aggregated precipitates of protein to disassociate. For this reason, it is recommended that the boil be kept to less than three hours and that boiling with hops not exceed ninety minutes.

Some breweries are equipped with stack condensers to be used in a "closed" boiling system. They are designed to precipitate out steam and protein solids and remove them from the boiling wort. In a closed system, this is accomplished as the barm or head pushes up into the condenser unit and is then removed by condensation. Any brewer who has skimmed the initial protein break from a kettle as it reaches a boil understands that these solids that are discarded are something best left out of the wort, and therefore out of the finished beer. Stack condensers can help facilitate this protein removal in much the same way. But these stack condensers, if not properly designed, can also be a deterrent to achieving an adequate boil. If designing a brew kettle, be sure that the heating surfaces of the kettle are properly sized and will not impede boiling or achieving the proper amount of wort evaporation.

Hop Bitterness: Extraction and Isomerization

Hops give bitterness and flavor to the wort. The bitterness comes from iso-alpha-acids, which are derived in the course of the boil from the alpha acids of the hops. Alpha acids are not very water soluble and must be boiled in order to isomerize them or make them water (wort) soluble. But the isomerization process is not solely heat dependent; it is enhanced by physical action as well. The maximum conversion of alpha acids to iso-alpha-acids is about 32 to 35%, and is best achieved with an approximately ninety-minute boil. Most homebrewers, incidentally, can expect 20 to 30% hop utilization. Boiling with hops for more than ninety minutes can extract harsh and unpleasant bitterness. Extended boiling can result in iso-alpha-acids being hydrolyzed to a nonbitter compound called humulinic, thereby lessening their effectiveness. When using longer boil times often associated with the brewing of barley wines, be prepared to hold off on adding your hops until later in the boil.

Another consideration when making high-gravity beers is that, as the gravity of the wort being produced increases, the hop utilization will decrease. We therefore suggest adding 1 to 4% more boiling hops into the kettle when brewing a barley wine. For example, use an additional 1% for a wort of 1.080 SG (20 °Plato) and 4% more for those massive gravities over 1.100 SG (25 °Plato).

Kettle pH

The kettle wort pH should be between 5.2 to 5.4 because this will favor protein coagulation and keep color formation at a low level. The optimum pH for protein coagulation is 5.2. Also a pH of 5.2 or above favors hop utilization and reduces harsh hop bitterness. If your kettle pH is too high, try adding gypsum to acidify it.

Color Formation

Boiling the wort produces an increase in color. The longer the boil, the more caramelization of sugars and the greater the formation of melanoidins, resulting in more color in the finished beer. Extended boils magnify the color representation of pale and specialty malts in particular, demanding the brewer use an even hand in their selection and proportion. Percentages of darker malts must be cut back compared to smaller beers with shorter boil times, in order that their presence enhance, not overwhelm, the color (and flavor) of the finished barley wine. This is of particular concern when trying to produce a lighter-colored or pale barley wine.

Evaporation

One way to enhance the original gravity of your beer is through evaporation. The longer the wort is boiled, the more water will evaporate out in the form of steam, and the more concentrated your wort will become. This will result in a higher gravity, and in barley wine brewing, this a good thing. We recommend boiling a barley wine for 2 to 2 1/2 hours. With a good rolling boil, yielding an evaporation rate of 8 to 12% per hour, gravity can be increased from the end of runoff by 2.5 to 5 °Plato (i.e., from 17 up to 21 or 22 °Plato). The rate of evaporation can be further increased by agitating the wort during the boil. Agitated (or swept) kettles are used in systems that have low heat exchange surface to liquid volume ratios. The concept of a swept kettle is to achieve continuous wort flow over the heat exchange surface, thus bringing a greater amount of liquid in contact with the heating surface.

The question becomes, how do you know if you are getting a boil that is sufficient to achieve the desired amount of wort concentration, properly stabilize your beer, and efficiently extract bitterness from your hops? The easiest way to measure the efficiency of your boil is by measuring the evaporation rate. This is easily done by taking a volume measurement in the kettle just prior to boiling and then again at the end of the boil. The difference is the number of barrels (or gallons) that went up your kettle stack (or into your kitchen) as evaporation. Take that number, divide it by the barrels (or gallons) you started with, and you end up with a percentage representing total evaporation. Divide total evaporation by the number of hours boiled and that is the rate of evaporation per hour. Eight to 12% evaporation per hour is desirable. If you are able to achieve 10 or 11%, you are doing better than many commercial microbreweries.

For example, if you start with 37 barrels (prior to boiling) and have 32 barrels at the end of the boil, then the difference is 5 barrels. Divide 5 barrels by the number of barrels before the boil (37) to arrive at .135, or 13.5% total evaporation. Then divide 13.5% by the length of the boil (1.5 hours, which gives you 9, or 9% evaporation per hour.

Finishing Hops

Unlike the systems devised for the measurement of boiling hops (international bittering units [IBUs] or alpha acid units [AAUs]), there is no good quantitative system to help in the selection of hops to be used for late additions or as finishing hops. Conventional brewing wisdom dictates certain varieties as being particularly suitable for additions of flavor and aroma. Whether the varieties used are traditional or newfangled, finishing hops should always be chosen subjectively for their flavor and aroma. One of the best ways to tell if a particular variety of hops will work for you is to take a couple of hop cones or pellets, rub them between your palms, and then take a good whiff. This will give you an idea of what the hop aroma will be like in your final product, and whether you like it.

Finishing hops can be added to the kettle either at or toward the end of the boil or they can be added to the whirlpool or the hop back. The whirlpool (or swirl tank) is a cylindrical vessel large enough to hold the entire post-boil wort. The hopped wort is run or pumped tangentially into the tank, causing it to swirl around. The rotational momentum causes the solid matter (hops and trub) to gather in a cone-shaped pile on the bottom of the tank. The clear wort is then drawn off from the side.

The hop back is a smaller vessel (usually 5 to 20% the size of the kettle volume) fitted with a screen in the bottom that acts as a strainer. The strainer catches the hop flowers as the wort is drained from the kettle. The brewer can also put dry flower hops into the hop back to extract and capture the maximum amount of the hops' volatile aromatic component. This is not the same as "dry hopping," which involves hop additions in the fermenter, conditioning vessel, or cask. In recent years the hop back has lost practical favor to whirlpools in breweries where pellet hops are more frequently used. Some brewers, however, believe that nothing is as effective in adding fragile hop aromas as the hop back.

Pitching the Yeast

It is a good idea to have your yeast prepared and ready to pitch (add to the cooled wort) before the end of the boil. A good healthy ale yeast culture will be needed, preferably one from a recent fermentation because that yeast will be freshest and strongest. We do not recommend brewing a barley wine with a yeast culture's first generation, but if you must use a new culture, make sure you grow a good strong starter so that there will be enough yeast to achieve the proper pitching rate. It is extremely important to pitch enough yeast in any brew, and this is especially true with barley wines. The proper pitching rate for any beer is one million cells per milliliter per degree Plato. So, for a 23 °Plato barley wine (1.092), you will need 23 million healthy yeast cells per milliliter in your pitched wort. That's a lot of yeast.

It is also important to ensure that the yeast you are using is alive and healthy. This can be done quickly and easily by a methylene blue staining test. Without pitching a sufficient quantity of healthy yeast, you will not get proper attenuation, and the resulting beer will be too sweet.

Every professional brewer or serious homebrewer should have access to a microscope and hemocytometer (used for counting yeast cells in a sample). These instruments will allow you to check the pitching rate and the viability of the yeast. If you don't have access to a microscope and a hemocytometer, we advise 1 1/2 to 2 times the regular pitching volume or weight that would normally be used for a beer of 13 °Plato (1.052) original gravity. Again, your best bet is to use yeast from a recent fermentation that went well or a properly grown-up (two- or three-step) starter from a packet of liquid yeast. When making high-gravity beers, it is always better to overpitch than to underpitch. One must significantly overpitch to see obvious negative effects.

There are also times when more yeast must be pitched, like when a disappointing hemocytometer reading is taken or when fermentation simply slows down. It is therefore advisable to have more healthy yeast on hand than went into the original brew. Keep this surplus yeast chilled and ready to go in the event of a sluggish fermentation. In professional breweries this is not ordinarily a problem, but in most cases homebrewers pitch all the yeast their starter has yielded. A second, or backup, starter may seem overly fussy, but it can be just the thing to jump-start a slow fermentation.

Knock Out (Casting Back) and Cooling the Wort

The wort is cooled as with other beers, but because of the greater amount of malt and hops used, it is highly likely that there will be more cold break (trub) to settle out. This can be removed in the whirlpool or by letting the hot wort stand in the kettle for fifteen to thirty minutes before knocking out (casting back) into a fermenter. An option for ensuring greater trub removal is to knock out into a clean fermenter and let the wort sit for an hour or two before drawing the trub off the bottom (if you have cylindroconical fermenters) or transferring the beer to another fermenter, leaving the trub behind. Naturally there are risks involved in transferring unfermented beer between vessels—sanitation must be above reproach. Increasing the number of surfaces that come in contact with the wort always increases the risk of infection.

It is important to make sure you get the proper amount of oxygen (or air) into the wort as you send the wort to the fermenter or cast back (see chapter 3). Without enough oxygen, the beer will not fully attenuate, and may not sufficiently begin fermenting. If you have a good temperature control on your fermenter, cast back at or just above your maximum desired fermentation temperature. The initial higher temperature may help get the fermentation started. We suggest that the fermentation should run between 66 to 72 °F (19 to 22 °C). If you do not have an accurate temperature control on your fermenter (as with many homebrew systems), we suggest you send the wort back 2 to 6 °F (-17 to -14 °C)—depending on the ambient temperature—below the maximum desired fermentation temperature. You will then have to watch the fermentation temperature carefully.

Fermentation

Fermentation is an exothermic reaction and temperatures can climb quickly. High-gravity beers can work themselves into an overheated frenzy if left to their own devices. You don't want your fermentation to run too warm. High-*gravity* fermentations will naturally

Copper square fermenters.

produce a greater amount of esters. Higher-*temper-ature* fermentations will exaggerate this phenome-non, producing both more esters and higher alcohol. Combining the two (high-gravity and high-temperature fermentations) can create some pretty strange-tasting beers.

We recommend that fermentation temperature be kept between 66 and 72 °F (19 and 22 °C). This of course is dependent on the yeast strain used—some ale yeast strains will work perfectly fine at tempera-tures as low as 60 °F (16 °C). But you do want to have some of those ale yeast esters and characters in your beer so don't ferment at too low a temperature even if your yeast is capable of doing so. It is also doubtful that at lower temperatures your fermentation would be completed. It is important to keep the fermenting beer in a temperature range that is not so high that it will produce excessive esters and not so low that the yeast quits fermenting.

As fermentation progresses, you may need to rouse (or stir up) the yeast to help keep the fermentation going. Studies have shown that periodically agitating the beer to keep the yeast in suspension speeds up fermentation and achieves greater attenuation. Rousing or agitation can be done in a variety of clean and careful ways if you have an open fermenter, but the easiest way is to blow carbon dioxide (CO_2) in through the bottom valve. It is also possible to rouse by using a sterilized pump. By pumping the yeast and wort from the bottom of the tank onto the top, you can get the yeast back into suspension. This should be done at low speed and with a minimum of splashing. For smaller homebrew batches, the yeast can be roused manually by agitating the fermenting vessel. With some highly flocculant strains, keeping the yeast in suspension will be the key to achieving desired terminal gravity.

Once the initial, or active, fermentation is finished, let the beer rest "warm," at or around fermentation temperature, for another seven to ten days. This will allow the yeast to completely attenuate the beer as well as to reduce diacetyl and other metabolic by-products of fermentation. It is worth noting that British malt is higher in the amino nutrients that can result in higher diacetyl levels, so this "warm" rest becomes even more important when using British malt. After the diacetyl rest is complete, chill the beer for aging.

Cold Aging

When the warm rest is complete, chill the beer to 32 to 52 °F (0 to 11 °C) for cold aging. This stage should last from one to three months, depending on the time and equipment you are able to devote to it. Most brewers agree that for barley wines to achieve maximum flavor development, aging with the yeast still in the fermenter is fairly important. You do not, for example, want to cold-crash your beer and then immediately filter it. The question then becomes, for how long and on how much yeast? We feel that after chilling the beer, it is best to let it go for a week or so before trying to remove any of the yeast. After that time you will want to chill the tank to below 40 °F (4 °C) and remove as much of the precipitated yeast as possible. The colder aging temperature helps minimize yeast autolysis and its negative effects.

You want to remove the yeast because starting around this time the yeast begins the process of self-digestion or autolysis. When this occurs the yeast releases enzymes that cause the decomposition and solubilization of macromolecules, organelles, and the cell wall. This allows the now soluble cell components to leak into the surrounding environment (your beer), resulting in a negative flavor impact. This "yeast bite" is often described as tasting yeasty or meaty. In a cylindroconical fermentation (uni) tank, you can draw yeast off from the bottom of the vessel. With other systems you will have to transfer the beer to a clean vessel, leaving the yeast sediment behind on the bottom. After the majority of the yeast has been removed, the aging process can continue for up to a year before packaging.

Filtration

Once fermentation has ended, the beer has been chilled, and the yeast sediment removed, it is time to decide if you want to filter the beer before it enters the long, slow, aging phase of its conditioning. Filtration removes haze-forming proteins, as well as yeast left in suspension, thus resulting in a bright and stable beer with cleaner and more defined flavor. But long periods of cold aging can bring these changes too. One problem with filtration is that it also removes other things from the beer—like color, flavor, body, hop bitterness, and hop aroma.

Is it necessary to filter a well-aged beer? We don't think so. We believe the proper amount of cold storage can leave a beer in better shape than filtration. But the problem is that the proper amount of aging varies greatly from beer to beer.

Aging times may exceed a year for some beers, and for commercial breweries it can be very costly to age a beer that long, to say nothing of the clutter that occurs when barley wine brewing time rolls around and you've still got the previous year's offering taking up tank space. It is also very difficult to keep your hands off a beer for that long, and the temptation is such that the whole batch could be "tasted off" before its scheduled release. But one must remember to be patient.

An alternative worth mentioning is pad filtration. A pad filter uses cellulose pads usually impregnated with diatomaceous earth (DE). These pads are produced in various grades (or porosity size). By using a pad that is fairly open, or of a high porosity, a brewer can remove some of the yeast and larger haze-forming protein complexes without stripping out too much of the desirable constituents that you want to remain in the beer. The filter pad that we have used with good results is the Schenk HS 6000 (formerly the AF 6000).

Packaging: Kegs vs. Bottles

There are several options for packaging a barley wine. The larger the package, the proportionately smaller the head space, and hence the lower oxygen-to-beer ratio. Oxygen is the foe of all packaged beers. Oxygen in a packaged beer can quickly degrade the flavors and stale the beer. This makes kegs a superior package for beer storage. But kegs are not always the most convenient packages to move, use, and store and it is nice to have smaller containers from which to sample. Always bottle at least some of your barley wine. This will allow you to take small taste samples and track its progress as it ages without having to compromise a larger quantity by tapping a whole keg. In addition, bottles of barley wine make great gifts for fellow brewers and beer writers who may be visiting your brewery.

Bottle Conditioning

Bottle conditioning is a more traditional way of packaging your beer and it is the easiest way to give some sparkle to your bottled beer at home. If done right, bottle conditioning will give a softer and more mellow carbonation than keg storage under pressure. Another benefit of bottle conditioning is that the yeast invariably present in the beer will scavenge whatever oxygen is present in the head space and metabolize it, keeping it from reacting with other components and causing staling.

There are certain difficulties associated with bottle conditioning high-gravity beers. Unlike other ales, barley wines have a very high alcohol content and are subject to long maturation periods prior to bottling. For these reasons, one cannot depend on the few worn-out yeast cells that might be in suspension to carbonate the beer. What this means is that you must dose with a measured amount of fresh and active yeast along with the primings. We have found that the best and easiest way to do this is to prime with actively fermenting wort, either from another fermenter that is at the proper stage of fermentation or with a yeast starter made specifically for this purpose. Our best results are achieved when we dose the entire amount to be bottled with fermenting wort and allow it a short time to mix before bottling. The actively fermenting wort should be at 10 °Plato (1.040) and have approximately 25 million yeast cells per milliliter in suspension. We recommend dosing with 4 to 6 liters fermenting wort per U.S. barrel of beer to be primed.

Once the primed beer has been bottled it will need to be stored at a relatively warm temperature (65 to 70 °F, 18 to 21 °C) for thirty or more days. Once it has warm conditioned enough for carbonation to build up, it should be stored again at a cooler temperature. Cellar temperatures—48 to 55 °F (9 to 13 °C)—are best. We recommend waiting at least 120 days after priming before partaking in this biggest of brews, your barley wine.

Laying Down the Beer (Cellaring)

Once the beer has been packaged it is time to put it away and give it any additional aging that the brewer feels it might need. Even though the beer may be drinkable (really quite drinkable) at this stage, there are some definite benefits gained by letting the beer continue to mature. The beer changes over time. How and how much it changes depends on a number of variables—gravity, hopping rate, hop variety, alcohol content, level of microbiological contamination, malt bill, oxygen present, cellaring temperature, and so forth. The beer should now be aged at cellar temperatures (48 to 56 °F, 9 to 13 °C) or below.

A growing body of evidence suggests that aging beer, like wine, is best done at cellar temperatures. Several brewers gave us information suggesting a barley wine aged at cellar temperatures will often have less of a sharp edge, a rounder, fuller character, and a more melded and cohesive flavor profile.

We have been able to put this hypothesis to the test over the last year and a half it took us to research and write this book. We found that many beers cellared over this period of time did indeed taste better than their counterparts that were held in cooler temperatures. Their flavors were more robust and round. We also found that some were not as clear or bright as those aged at lower temperatures and that this had a flavor impact as well. Additionally, we found that barley wine aged at temperatures above 60 °F (16 °C) did not fare as well as those aged at cellar temperatures, or below 48 °F (9 °C). We attributed this to the fact that chemical reactions are accelerated at higher temperatures. This may mean that beers cellared between 48 and 56 °F (9 and 13 °C) may not fare as well as those held at lower temperatures over the long haul. Our research (we are happy to say) is continuing in this area.

Our recommendation is to decrease the temperature of cellaring as the length of aging increases. For example if you are holding a case of Bigfoot, keep it at 50 °F (10 °C) for the first year or two. Then, if you are patient enough to have any left, move it to a cooler for the rest of its life. The higher gravity, less hoppy barley wine will do better with extended cellar temperature aging.

CHAPTER 5

Professional Barley Wine Breweries

There are currently over two hundred breweries in the world making these high-gravity brews, most of them in the United States. We could not hope to list them all but many American and Canadian ones are listed in appendix C. We solicited breweries around the U.S. and England for information on their barley wines and what follows is the information we compiled. We managed to obtain a fair amount of good technical data from some of our respondents, enough that we hope you will be able to gain some insights into their brewing process and their beers. Also our own tasting notes are included when possible.

We encourage you to try the barley wines available commercially. Trying them gives you a better appreciation and understanding of the style.

Bass No. 1 (1994)

Brewer: Bass
Original Gravity (OG): 1.096–1.120 (24–29 °Plato)
    throughout the years
Terminal Gravity (TG): Not available (N/A)
Alcohol by Volume (ABV): 10+%
International Bittering Units (IBUs): N/A (high hop
    to malt ratio) estimated about 60–70
Hop Variety: Fuggle and Golding
Malt: English two-row pale malt, invert sugar
Mash: 148–150 °F (66 °C)
Boil: 120+ minutes
Fermentation Temperature: 60–65 °F (16–18 °C)
Yeast: Bass Ale
Fermentation Time: N/A
Aging (prior to packaging): N/A

Notes: At first, this massive beer was produced year-round. Later, production was reduced to just once a year for the Christmas season. Now production is sporadic. Its last regular brewing was in 1995 and currently it is only produced in the museum brewery (7 to 8 British barrels at a time) located in the Bass plant in Burton-upon-Trent.

Bass No. 1 is a medium-dark beer that gets all its color from the boil. It is 100% pale malt with a small addition of invert sugar.

The 1994 vintage has a rich malt character without being too sweet. Caramellike. It has a slight sourness to the nose and is dry on the palate, but has a nice soft roundness and full, silky, smooth round body. Oaklike overtones are mixed with warming higher alcohols. Well-balanced with good hop flavor to match the strong malt character. This is a must-try barley wine, if it can be found.

Rudyard's Rare

Brewer: Rudyard S. Kipling, Hale's Ales Ltd.
OG: 1.090 (22.5 °Plato)
TG: 1.019 (4.75 °Plato)
ABV: 9.2%
IBUs: 63
Hop Variety: Nugget/Nugget
Malt: Great Western two-row pale, caramel 30 °L, black malt
Mash: 150 °F (66 °C) for 60 minutes
Boil: 60 minutes
Fermentation Temperature: 68–70 °F (20–21 °C)
Yeast: Hale's Ale
Fermentation Time: N/A
Aging (prior to packaging): N/A

Old Weasel

Brewer: Curt Anderson, Burlingame Station
OG: 1.093 (24.3 °Plato)
TG: 1.035 (8.7 °Plato)
ABV: 9%
IBUs: 66
Hop Variety: Galena and Columbus/Columbus,
   Liberty, Cascade
Malt: Pale two-row, Munich, brown, carastan 30 °L
Mash: 153 °F (67 °C)
Boil: 105 minutes
Fermentation Temperature: N/A
Yeast: British Ale
Fermentation Time: N/A
Aging (prior to packaging): N/A

Notes: A 1995 Great American Beer Festival (GABF) bronze medal winner. Nutty caramel aroma, low hop aroma, pineapple and apricot esters derived from the combination of the hops and the yeast. The hop bitterness is strong and lingers.

Bigfoot

Brewer: Sierra Nevada
OG: 1.092 (23.0 °Plato)
TG: 1.024 (6.0 °Plato)
ABV: 8.95%*
IBUs: 82.5

Hop Variety: Nugget/Cascade (Cascade and
    Centennial dry hop)
Malt: Two-row pale, caramel
Mash: N/A
Boil: 3 hours
Fermentation Temperature: N/A
Yeast: Ale
Fermentation Time: N/A
Aging (prior to packaging): N/A

Notes: Gold at the 1987, 1988, 1992, 1995 GABF.
Wow! Amazingly good (and consistent) beer. Really
rather light in color considering the length of the boil.
This beer is extremely hoppy and yet has a good stiff
malt backing. The malt character is not as complex as
some barley wines, yet it mixes nicely with the yeast
esters and flavors, which are clean and dry. Many
agree that the 1995 barley wine is the best yet. This is
a great beer.

    **Sierra Nevada's literature says 10.1 ABV, but, given
the original and terminal gravities, by our calculations
that would be a slight stretch.*

Golden Pride

Brewer: Fuller's
OG: 1.086 (21.5 °Plato)
TG: 1.020 (5.0 °Plato)
ABV: 8.5%

IBUs: 38
Hop Variety: N/A
Malt: All pale malt
Mash: Single infusion
Boil: N/A
Fermentation Temperature: 68–70 °F (20–21 °C)
Yeast: Fuller's
Fermentation Time: N/A
Aging (prior to packaging): N/A

Notes: First brewed in 1967 as a dark strong ale, but in the 1970s the taste for darker ale began to wane and Fuller's changed it to a golden amber color. This beer is brewed with the parti-gyle system, with the second runnings going on to become the Chiswick bitter. It has been a great success for Fuller's and has grown to 0.5% of their total production.

Beowulf's Bark
Brewer: Sean Donnelly and Teri Fahrendorf,
  Steelhead Brewing Company
OG: 1.092 (23.7 °Plato)
TG: 1.021 (5.3 °Plato)
ABV: 9.66%
IBUs: 68
Hop Variety: Chinook/Centennial, Mt. Hood,
  Cascade
Malt: Two-row pale, crystal 80 °L and 130 °L,

chocolate, CaraPils, Munich
Mash: 153 °F (67 °C) for 60 minutes
Boil: 90 minutes
Fermentation Temperature: 72 °F (22 °C)
Yeast: Ale
Fermentation Time: 28 days
Aging (prior to packaging): N/A

Road House

Brewer: Charles Martinez, Broadway Brewing Company
OG: 1.104 (26 °Plato)
TG: 1.026 (6.4 °Plato)
ABV: 10.3%
IBUs: 78
Hop Variety: Columbus/centennial and cascade
Malt: Two-row pale, Munich, crystal 130 °L and 30
  °L, brown, chocolate, special roast
Mash: 151 °F (66 °C)
Boil: 2.5 hours
Fermentation Temperature: N/A
Yeast: Ale
Fermentation Time: N/A
Aging (prior to packaging): N/A

Notes: Slight caramel nose with overtones of prune
and a hint of sourness (the good kind). Good flavors,
nice hop bitterness, not cloying, with a dry finish.
This is a well-balanced beer with a nice maltiness.

Old Possum

Brewer: James Ottolini, Saint Louis Brewery
OG: 1.082 (20.5 °Plato)
TG: 1.020 (5.0 °Plato)
ABV: 8.15%
IBUs: N/A
Hop Variety: Perle, Eroica/Kent Golding
Malt: Two-row pale, caramel 10 °L and 50 °L, wheat, chocolate, black
Mash: 154 °F (68 °C)
Boil: N/A
Fermentation Temperature: N/A
Yeast: N/A
Fermentation Time: N/A
Aging (prior to packaging): N/A

Monster (1996)

Brewer: Garrett Oliver, Brooklyn Brewery
OG: 1.096 (24.0 °Plato)
TG: 1.015 (3.8 °Plato)
ABV: 10.5%
IBUs: 80
Hop Variety: Willamette (boil), Cascade, Fuggle
Malt: 50% Marris Otter pale malt, 23% Halcyon pale malt, 23% Pipkin pale malts, 2% wheat, 1.5% crystal, less than 0.5% chocolate malt
Mash: 3 to 1 (water to malt) infusion mash 90 minutes at 149 °F (65 °C), ramped up to 158 °F (70 °C) over 10 minutes, held there for 20

minutes. Mash out at 168 °F (76 °C). Three-hour, 20-minute runoff.

Boil: 105 minutes

Fermentation Temperature: 63–69 °F (17–21 °C)

Yeast: English ale (Wyeast 1068)

Fermentation Time: 7 days (crash-chilled to 52 °F [11 °C] after 7 days)

Aging (prior to packaging): 3 months

Notes: Whoa! Rich and complex malt backbone with a good hop balance. Nice bitterness and flavor without being overdone. The hop aroma is light and subdued. Plenty of alcohol warming and enjoyable yeast flavor. A very well-balanced barley wine. You could (and we did) have several servings. This beer is in the middle of the West Coast and English styles (in geography and flavor). A really good barley wine.

Old Gander

Brewer: Mike Hartman, Sleeping Lady Brewing Company

OG: 1.090 (22.5 °Plato)

TG: 1.038 (9.4 °Plato)

ABV: 6.9

IBUs: 75

Hop Variety: Chinook/Perle, Cascade

Malt: German two-row, Munich, crystal 80 °L, carastan, wheat, light malt extract, light brown sugar

Mash: 156 °F (69 °C)

Boil: 90 minutes
Fermentation Temperature: 68 °F (20 °C)
Yeast: Whitbread Ale
Fermentation Time: 21 days
Aging (prior to packaging): 3 months

Pyramid Anniversary Ale (1995)

Brewer: Clay Biberdorf, Pyramid Ales Brewery
OG: 1.096 (24.0 °Plato)
TG: 1.022 (5.5 °Plato)
ABV: 9.7%
IBUs: 80 (est.)
Hop Variety: Kent Golding/Target
Malt: Great western two-row, H.B. crystal malt (80 °L)
Mash: 122 °F (50 °C) for 30 minutes and 155 °F
  (68 °C) for 90 minutes
Boil: 90 minutes
Fermentation Temperature: 68 °F (20 °C)
Yeast: Pyramid Ale
Fermentation Time: N/A
Aging (prior to packaging): 8 months

Notes: Caramel flavors, strong maltiness mixed with higher alcohols. Candied orange overtones.

Old Foghorn (1996)

Brewer: Anchor Brewing Company
OG: 1.100 (25 °Plato)
TG: N/A

ABV: N/A
IBUs: N/A
Hop Variety: N/A
Malt: N/A (Billed as, "Three times the malt as a normal brew.")
Mash: N/A
Boil: N/A
Fermentation Temperature: N/A
Yeast: Ale
Fermentation Time: 2–3 weeks, then "kept on the yeast for 9 months"
Aging (prior to packaging): Minimum of 9 months

Notes: First brewed in 1975 and is dry hopped. Anchor Brewing volunteers so little information on their beers that one begins to feel as if the beer is brewed by some secret monastic order. Dark caramel color. Good malt flavor. Hoppy without being over-powering. It has a very nice balance.

Old Bawdy Barley Wine (1994)

Brewer: Pike Brewing Company
OG: 1.098 (24.5 °Plato)
TG: 1.016 (4 °Plato)
ABV: 10.75%
IBUs: 87–90
Hop Variety: Varies with year (lots of American hops)
Malt: Lightly peated Scottish malt, Marris Otter

two-row, crisp crystal
Mash: 150 °F (66 °C) for 90 minutes
Boil: 120 minutes
Fermentation Temperature: 70–72 °F (21–22 °C)
Yeast: Pike Place Ale
Fermentation Time: 14 days
Aging (prior to packaging): 90 days

Notes: This beer is slightly different each year, as the brewery changes both the percentages in the malt bill and the varieties of hops. Won GABF bronze medal in 1993 and silver in 1994. The beer is named Old Bawdy because the original Pike Place Brewery was housed in a former brothel (or bawdy house). It has a complex malt flavor reminiscent of hearty dark bread, with a hint of peat smoke character in the background. Big hop flavor and bitterness. The bitterness is strong but not harsh. The beer carries flavors of apricot, peach, and pineapple from the yeast and higher alcohols. Round and full but with a definite bitterness.

Thomas Hardy (1989)
Brewer: Thomas Hardy Brewery (formerly Eldridge Pope Brewery)
OG: 1.124 (31 °Plato)
TG: 1.034 (10.75 °Plato)
ABV: 12% ("stated," but 10.6% by our calculation)

IBUs: 50
Hop Variety: Northdown, Challenger, Golding
Malt: Pipkin pale two-row, sugar
Mash: First running only
Boil: 90 minutes
Fermentation Temperature: 68 °F (20 °C)
Yeast: Bavarian lager yeast (Yes, we asked twice to
    be sure we heard them right.)
Fermentation Time: 90 days (initial ferment 7–10 days)
Aging (prior to packaging): 6 months

Notes: The Eldridge Pope Brewery has been in operation since the 1830s. In 1968, the Thomas Hardy Society approached this Dorchester brewery and asked them to brew an ale to commemorate the fortieth anniversary of Mr. Hardy's demise. They hoped the hometown brewery could re-create the brew the famous author had written about so eloquently. The beer was to be a one-off but became so popular that it was made into a regular brew.

The beer is made with 100% pale malt to a gravity of 1.128 and 12% ABV. The hops are Kent Golding and Fuggle (and lots of them). The beer gets multiple yeast pitchings (three to four) over a six-month period prior to bottling. Although the brewery used ale yeast in the earlier versions, they now ferment the barley wine with a lager yeast. The beer goes into the bottle unfiltered, unpasteurised, and unprimed. The beer is vintage-dated and the brewery recommends that the beer be laid down for a minimum of five years.

In taste testings of several years, we found considerable variation between years, in flavor as well as in the condition of the beer. Most years were rather lackluster. The best by far was the 1989. It was truly a wonderful year.

The 1989 is in nice condition. The nose is port/sherrylike with a hint of sourness. It has a reddish brown cherry hue. It is firm and robust with a slightly salty flavor. It has complex, sweet, currant, and cherry flavors with a hint of woodiness. Great lingering finish. This is the beer we have heard so much about.

Southern Oregon and Pacific Brewing Company's Barley Wine

Brewer: Hubert Smith, Southern Oregon and Pacific Brewing Company

OG: 1.099 (24.75 °Plato)

TG: 1.022 (5.5)

ABV: 10.1%

IBUs: 80

Hop Variety: Cascade, Chinook, Fuggle

Malt: G.W. Kent two-row pale, H. B. Munich

Mash: 150 °F (66 °C) for 90 minutes

Boil: 2 hours

Fermentation Temperature: 68 °F (20 °C)

Yeast: Nottingham ale yeast (live, active)

Fermentation Time: N/A
Aging (prior to packaging): 8 months (cold)

Adambier

Brewer: Hair of the Dog Brewery
OG: 1.094 (23.5 °Plato)
TG: 1.020 (5.0 °Plato)
ABV: 9.9%
IBUs: 65
Hop Variety: Northern Brewer, Tettnang
Malt: A blend of six varieties of malt: pale, Munich, crystal, chocolate, black patent, and a dash of Scottish peated
Mash: N/A
Boil: 2 hours
Fermentation Temperature: 68–70 °F (20–21 °C)
Yeast: German ale yeast
Fermentation Time: 3 to 4 days
Aging (prior to packaging): N/A

Notes: Dog bites man. In 1996, voted "domestic beer of the year" by the *Malt Advocate* and one of the "ten best beers of the year" by the *Wine Enthusiast* magazine. It is an amazingly complex and rich beer. John Hansell (publisher of the *Malt Advocate*) calls it "reckless, assertive, enjoyably complex and silky smooth." The idea for Adambier came from the 1889 book *The Curiosities of Ale and Beer* which tells of King

Frederick of Prussia's visit to Dortmund. Upon his arrival, he was offered a large tankard of their very best ale. He drank it down in one draught, promptly passed out, and did not awaken for more than 24 hours. The beer, which was made locally, was a dark, rich, very strong ale called Adambier, laid down to age for 10 years in oaken barrels. The Hair of the Dog guys have done an admirable job of reproducing this beer. It has a rich malty aroma with a hint of candy sugar, and is smooth, creamy, full-bodied, with fruity and hop overtones. There are also some peaty whiskeylike flavors, too.

Cyclops (Old One Eye)

Brewer: Elysian Brewing
OG: 1.106 (25 °Plato)
TG: 1.021 (5.25 °Plato)
ABV: 10%
IBUs: 65
Hop Variety: Chinook, Centennial, Cascade
Malt: American two-row pale, Munich, crystal 56 °L, caramalt 11 °L
Mash: 150 °F (66 °C) for 90 minutes
Boil: 120 minutes
Fermentation Temperature: 68–70 °F (20–21 °C)
Yeast: Ale
Fermentation Time: 14 days
Aging (prior to packaging): 6 months

Notes: Extreme tropical fruit esters, lots of alcohol, including higher alcohols, and strong malt character. Good hop balance.

Prize Old Ale

Brewer: George Gale and Company, Ltd.
OG: 1.091 (22.8 °Plato)
TG: 1.014 (3.5 °Plato)
ABV: 10%
IBUs: N/A (low)
Hop Variety: Fuggle, Golding, Challanger
Malt: Marris Otter two-row pale, black malt, caramel
Mash: 150 °F (66 °C) for 90 minutes
Boil: 120 minutes
Fermentation Temperature: 62–70 °F (17–21 °C)
Yeast: Ale
Fermentation Time: 21 days (in wood fermenters)
Aging (prior to packaging): 12 months

Notes: This beer was first brewed over 70 years ago and is still made with the same equipment. This beer really is an "old ale" as the name says, but one cannot talk about high-gravity beers and their history without mentioning Gale's Prize Old Ale—it is probably one of the most authentic representations of the style. An amazingly complex and wonderful beer, it has a huge fruit aroma and palate, backed by strong yet mellow malt character. There is a slight acidity either from the oak or from a slight bacterial ferment (the brewers deny the presence of bacteria or foreign yeast). This is a beer that really stands alone in today's beer world. If you can find a bottle, buy it.

Glacier Brewhouse Barley Wine

Brewer: Shawn Wendling, Glacier Brewhouse
OG: 1.102 (25.5 °Plato)
TG: 1.021 (5.2 °Plato)
ABV: 11.5%
IBUs: 90
Hop Variety: Columbus
Malt: 36% Gambrinus two-row pale, 36% Great Western NWPA two-row, 14% Great Western Munich, 5% Special B, 6% honey malt, 4% torrified wheat
Mash: 152 °F (67 °C) for 90 minutes
Boil: 3 hours
Fermentation Temperature: N/A
Yeast: Wyeast 1728 (Scottish Ale)
Fermentation Time: N/A
Aging (prior to packaging): 3 months (cold) and 3-plus months in new oak casks (giving it "vanilla oak overtones and some bourbon-esque qualities")

Notes: "This year the Barley wine fermented violently. At one point we had to lash down the fermenter and flood the containment area around its base to prevent meltdown or damage to the superstructure" (Brewer's Log).

Special Old Ale

Brewer: Jeff Charnick, Commonwealth Brewery
OG: 1.090 (22.3 °Plato)
TG: N/A
ABV: N/A
IBUs: N/A
Hop Variety: Yakima Golding, East Kent Golding
Malt: Pale ale malt, Special B, CaraPils, cane sugar
Mash: 158 °F (70 °C) for 90 minutes
Boil: 150 minutes
Fermentation Temperature: 68 °F (20 °C)
Yeast: Fuller's
Fermentation Time: N/A
Aging (prior to packaging): 12 months

Notes: Nice vinous, old ale character, especially in an older version of some 18 months; it is dark, but not opaque.

CHAPTER 6

Recipes

The recipes that follow are from a wide range of brewers and brewing backgrounds. We have tried to get an interesting cross section of the brewing community to share their ideas and recipes with us. Some of the brewers you may recognize, others you may not. We thought the wide range of ideas would be more interesting than our personal tired old homebrew recipes. Some of the procedures in the following recipes may go against the recommendations made in this (or other) books—there are few absolutes in brewing, as long as the beer tastes good. What works for one brewer may not be the answer for all brewers. Experimentation is the way to innovation and (possibly) making a great beer. The views or procedures expressed in the following recipes are from the brewers themselves. All of the recipes are for either 5 gallons or 1 barrel.

Note: We suggest that when homebrewing you always make a yeast starter.

Tsampa Barley Wine

Brewer: Clay Biberdorf, head brewer, Pyramid Brewing, Kalama, Washington

Malt	5 Gallons	1 Barrel
Pale two-row	11 lb.	66 lb.
Crystal (60 °L)	0.5 lb.	3 lb.
Munich malt	0.5 lb.	3 lb.
Alexander Sun Country unhopped malt extract	4 lb.	24 lb.
Dry malt extract	3 lb.	18 lb.

Hops	5 Gallons	1 Barrel
Eroica pellets (60 min.) (11.8 AAU)	1 oz.	6 oz.
Galena pellets (50 min.) (12.0 AAU)	1 oz.	6 oz.
Eroica pellets (40 min.)	1 oz.	6 oz.
Galena pellets (30 min.)	1 oz.	6 oz.
Hallertauer flower (5 min.) (2.7 AAU)	1 oz.	6 oz.

Dry Hop		
E. Kent Golding	1 oz.	6 oz.
Hallertau	1 oz.	6 oz.
Tettnang	1 oz.	6 oz.

Barley Wine Specifications

Mash:	122 °F (50 °C) for 35 minutes, 155 °F (68 °C) for 80 minutes, 168 °F (76 °C) for 15 minutes. Sparge until last runnings are 2.25 °Plato.
Boil:	60 minutes
OG:	26 °Plato
TG:	7.5 °Plato
Ferment Temp.:	66 °F (19 °C)

Yeast:	Equal parts Brewer's Choice dried yeast and Montrachet champagne dried yeast
Ferment Time:	5 days
Aging (prior to packaging):	30 days
Aging in the bottle:	1–2 years

Batch 100: Barley Wine

Brewer: Ray Daniels, author, fanatic homebrewer, and Mr. Real Ale America

Malt	5 Gallons	1 Barrel
Marris Otter pale malt	10 lb.	60 lb.
Light malt extract	4.5 lb.	27 lb.
Dark wheat malt	3 lb.	18 lb.
Belgian biscuit malt	3 lb.	18 lb.
Crystal malt (80 °L)	1 lb.	6 lb.
CaraPils malt	1 lb.	6 lb.
CaraMunich malt	1 lb.	6 lb.

Hops	5 Gallons	1 Barrel
Chinook (60 min.)	1.5 oz.	9 oz.
Perle (60 min.)	1 oz.	6 oz.
Cascade (15 min.)	1.5 oz.	9 oz.
Northern Brewer (5 min.)	1 oz.	6 oz.
Cascade (5 min.)	1 oz.	6 oz.

Barley Wine Specifications

Mash:	150 °F (66 °C) for 90 minutes (add extract at boil)
Boil:	2 hours
IBUs:	100 (est.)
OG:	25 °Plato (1.102)
TG:	8 °Plato (1.032)
ABV:	8.95%

Ferment Temp.:	64–68 °F (18–20 °C)
Yeast:	Ale
Ferment Time:	Primary 15 days, secondary 15–30 days
Aging (prior to packaging):	2 years

Malzwein Alt Barley Wine ("German Experiment")

Brewer: Charlie Papazian, godfather of the American home-brewing revolution

Malt	5 Gallons	1 Barrel
Light dry malt extract	12 lb.	72 lb.
Pale malt	2.5 lb.	15 lb.
Munich malt	2 lb.	12 lb.
Crystal malt	1 lb.	6 lb.
Dextrin malt	0.5 lb.	3 lb.
Special roast or aromatic malt	0.5 lb.	3 lb.

Hops	5 Gallons	1 Barrel
German Northern Brewer (60 min.)	6 oz.	36 oz.
German Hallertau (10 min.)	1.5 oz.	9 oz.
Saaz (end of boil)	1.5 oz.	9 oz.

Barley Wine Specifications

Mash:	For 5 gallons mix 6.5 quarts 130 °F (54 °C) water with crushed malt and hold at 122 °F (50 °C) for 30 minutes. Add 3.5 quarts boiling water, hold at 152–155 °F (67–68 °C) for 60 minutes. Mash out to 165 °F (74 °C). Sparge with 3 gallons. Add extract and boil. At the end of the boil let the wort cool to 110 °F (43 °C) then add to 3 gallons of chilled 50 °F (10 °C) water. Let stand until it is 70 °F (21 °C). Pitch yeast.

For 1 barrel mix 39 quarts 130 °F (54 °C) water with crushed malt and hold at 122 °F (50 °C) for 30 minutes. Add 21 quarts boiling water, hold at 152–155 °F (67–68 °C) for 60 minutes. Mash out to 165 °F (74 °C). Sparge with 18 gallons. Add extract and boil. At the end of the boil let the wort cool to 110 °F (43 °C) then add to 18 gallons of chilled 50 °F (10 °C) water, let stand until it is 70 °F (21 °C). Pitch yeast.

Boil:	90 minutes
IBUs:	50–70
OG:	24.5–27 °Plato (1.098–1.108)
TG:	6.5–8 °Plato (1.028–1.032)
ABV:	8.9–10.5%
Ferment Temp.:	66–70 °F (19–21 °C)
Yeast:	American ale yeast 1056
Ferment Time:	3–7 days
Aging (prior to packaging):	3–4 weeks
Aging after bottling:	90+ days

Barley Wine

Brewers: George and Laurie Fix, brewers, authors, beer fanatics

Malt	5 Gallons	1 Barrel
British pale two-row malt	20 lb.	120 lb.
British crystal malt (120 °L)	2.5 lb.	15 lb.

Hops	5 Gallons	1 Barrel
Columbus (13% AA)	1 oz.	6 oz.
First Gold (8% AA)	1 oz.	6 oz.

Barley Wine Specifications

Mash: For 5 gallons, mix 7 gallons of 104 °F (40 °C) water with crushed pale malt and hold for 30 minutes. Add 3 gallons of boiling water and the crystal malt mix and hold for 15 minutes at approximately 140 °F (60 °C). Slowly raise to 158 °F (70 °C) and hold for 15 minutes. Raise to 167 °F (75 °C) and hold for 10 minutes. Run off all the liquid and do not sparge. Collect approximately 7 gallons of wort.

For 1 barrel, mix 42 gallons of 104 °F (40 °C) water with crushed pale malt and hold for 30 minutes. Add 15 gallons boiling water and the crystal malt mix and hold for 15 minutes at approximately 140 °F (60 °C). Slowly raise to 158 °F (70 °C) and hold for 15 minutes. Raise to 158 °F (75 °C) and hold for 10 minutes. Run off all the liquid and do not sparge. Collect approximately 42 gallons of wort.

Boil:	Until there is a 10% volume reduction (approximately 1.5–2 hours)
Hop Addition:	Put the Columbus (13% AA) in before filling the kettle, add additional First Gold (8% AA) after 45 minutes of boiling.
IBUs:	70 mg/l
OG:	24 °Plato (1.096)
TG:	7 °Plato (1.028)
ABV:	8.9%
Ferment Temp.:	Ale temp.
Yeast:	White Lab WLP 001 (at a rate of 30 million cells/ml and 95% viability)
Ferment Time:	—
Aging (prior to packaging):	9–12 months

Black Blaggart Barley Wine

Brewer: A. F. Allen, unemployed keg washer who we picked up outside of Burton

Malt	5 Gallons	1 Barrel
English two-row pale malt	18 lb.	108 lb.
Munich malt	1 lb.	6 lb.
Crystal malt (80 °L)	1 lb.	6 lb.
Roasted barley	0.25 lb.	1.5 lb.

Hops	5 Gallons	1 Barrel
Chinook flower (90 min.) (12.1 AAU)	1 oz.	6 oz.
Perle flower (60 min.) (7.8 AAU)	1 oz.	6 oz.
Mt. Hood flower (5 min.)	1 oz.	6 oz.
Chinook flower (1 min.)	1 oz.	6 oz.

Barley Wine Specifications

Mash:	Infusion mash at 150 °F (66 °C) for 90 minutes
Boil:	120 minutes
OG:	1.098 (24.5 °Plato)
TG:	1.018 (4.5 °Plato)
ABV:	10.5%
Ferment Temp.:	70 °F (21 °C)
Yeast:	Pike Place yeast or London ale yeast
Ferment Time:	7 days
Aging (prior to packaging):	90 days
Aging in the bottle:	90+ days

Buffalo Bill's Barley Wine—
Brown Sugar (How Come You Taste So Good?)

Brewer: Bill Owens, publisher of *American Brewer*, photographer, "idea man"

Malt	5 Gallons	1 Barrel
Two-row pale malt	16.5 lb.	99 lb.
Crystal malt (120 °L)	1.6 lb.	9.5 lb.
Brown sugar	5.5 lb.	33 lb.

Hops	5 Gallons	1 Barrel
Cascade flower (90 min.) (69 IBU)	9 oz.	54 oz.
Cascade flower (end of boil)	8 oz.	48 oz.

Barley Wine Specifications

Mash:	Infusion mash at 158 °F (70 °C) for 90 minutes, sparge for 5 minutes, add the brown sugar to the kettle at the boil.
Boil:	90 minutes
OG:	23.75 °Plato
TG:	6–6.5 °Plato
ABV:	9.3%
Ferment Temp.:	70 °F (start at 70 °F [21 °C] down to 60 °F [16 °C] over 14 days). On the third day of fermentation, pump beer back onto itself to give the yeast fresh oxygen (and rouse the yeast), allowing the beer to ferment dry.
Yeast:	English ale yeast
Ferment Time:	14 days
Aging (prior to packaging):	30 days at 45–48 °F (7–9 °C)
Aging in the bottle:	One year, if possible

Oregon Adambier—A Barley Wine–Style Ale
Brewer: Fred Eckhardt, author, beer and saki statesman

Malt	5 Gallons	1 Barrel
Two-row pale malt	13.5 lb	81 lb.
Wheat malt	1.5 lb.	9 lb.
Munich malt	12 oz.	4.5 lb.
Dark caramel malt	12 oz.	4.5 lb.
Dark roasted barley	2 oz.*	12 oz.**

*Or two 3.3 lb. cans of German malt extract, 2 lb. crushed dark crystal malt, 2.5 oz. crushed dark roasted barley.

**Or twelve 3.3 lb. cans of German malt extract, 12 lb. crushed dark crystal malt, 15 oz. crushed dark roasted barley.

Hops	5 Gallons	1 Barrel
Perle (8–10% AA)		
(105 min.)	1.25 oz.	7.5 oz.
Perle (8–10% AA) (60 min.)	1.25 oz.	7.5 oz.
Tettnang (5 min.)	0.8 oz.	4.7 oz.
Tettnang (end of boil)	0.8 oz.	4.8 oz.

Barley Wine Specifications

Mash:	Water hardness about 1300 ppm with a Burton salts addition. Mash in two segments, use half the grain in each one.
Boil:	2 hours (or longer if needed to reach gravity)
IBUs:	About 40
OG:	22.4 °Plato (1.092)
TG:	4.9 °Plato (1.019)
ABV:	9.2%
Ferment Temp.:	Start ferment at 68–70 °F (20–21 °C) and at high krausen lower to 64 °F (18 °C)
Yeast:	German ale yeast (Wyeast 1007) from a strong,

Barley Wine

vigorous starter
Ferment Time: 4–5 days
Aging (prior to packaging): Lager at 41 °F (5 °C) for 21 days or until clear

Notes: "This is similar to the homebrew we did experimentally to see what
Adambier would be like. Adambier is that strong old Dortmunder altbier that
put Frederick the Great under the weather for a full day, in the mid-nineteenth
century. With no information available regarding ingredients in that nineteenth-century brew, we started with an altbier recipe and doubled it, for a
beginning Adam recipe, and worked from there, using an alt yeast and altbier
production methods (warm ferment, cold aging). This is not the same as the
recipe adopted by Portland's Hair of the Dog Brewery."—Fred

Sleepwalker Barley Wine

Brewer: Greg Noonan, author, head brewer and owner of the
Vermont Pub and Brewery and The Seven Barrel Brewery, all
around nice guy

Malt	5 Gallons	1 Barrel
Pale two-row malt	7.5 lb.	45 lb.
Wheat malt	1.5 lb.	9 lb.
Crystal malt	2.25 lb.	13.5 lb.
Light malt extract (add at boil)	4.4 lb.	27 lb.

Hops	5 Gallons	1 Barrel
Nugget (90 min.)	0.5 oz.	3 oz.
Nugget (45 min.)	0.75 oz.	4.5 oz.
Fuggle (end of boil)	1 oz.	3 oz.

Barley Wine Specifications

Mash:	60 minutes at 150 °F (66 °C)
Boil:	90 minutes
IBUs:	50
OG:	24 °Plato (1.096)
TG:	6 °Plato (1.024)
ABV:	9.4%
Ferment Temp.:	65–68 °F (18–20 °C)

Yeast:	Fruity ale yeast
Ferment Time:	3 days
Aging (prior to packaging):	30 days (7 days on 1oz. Fuggle hops, dry hopped)

Notes: Water treatment: 7.5 gallons of hard water to mash; 400 ppm total hardness by adding 125 ppm calcium, 25 ppm magnesium, 400 ppm sulfate (SO4). Aerate cooled wort well, keep the fermentation cool (68 °F [20 °C] or below) to favor ester production over higher alcohol production.

My Old Flame Barley Wine

Brewers: Randy Mosher, Mr. Homebrew and renowned beer author, and Ray Spangler

Malt	5 Gallons	1 Barrel
Pale two-row malt	5 lb.	30 lb.
Mild ale malt	8 lb.	48 lb.
Wheat malt	1 lb.	6 lb.
Pale malt		
(toasted for 20 min. at 350 °F)	1 lb.	6 lb.

Hops	5 Gallons	1 Barrel
Northern Brewer (90 min.)	2 oz.	12 oz.
Cascade (90 min.)	1 oz.	6 oz.
Tettnang (40 min.)	1.5 oz.	9 oz.
Golding (end of boil)	1 oz.	6 oz.
Cascade (end of boil)	0.5 oz.	3 oz.

Barley Wine Specifications

Mash:	Mash all malt in 1 quart of water per pound of malt for 1 hour at 158 °F (70 °C). Run off 6 gallons.
Boil:	2 hours
IBUs:	—
OG:	20.25 °Plato (1.081)
TG:	7.5 °Plato (1.030)
ABV:	6.7%
Ferment Temp.:	70 °F (21 °C)

Barley Wine

Yeast:	Ale
Ferment Time:	5–7 days
Aging (prior to packaging):	"Age it a year or more. I have some that go five years or more before starting to fall off. You just have to brew and brew, fill the basement with more barley wine than you'll ever need, then you have enough." —Randy and Ray

Barley Wine

Brewer: Kevin Forhan, head brewer at Big Time Brewery, left-wing radical

Malt	5 Gallons	1 Barrel
Lightly peated Scottish distiller malt	20 lb.	120 lb.
Crisp Marris Otter pale malt	10 lb.	60 lb.
Homemade crystal malt	2 lb.	12 lb.

Hops	5 Gallons	1 Barrel
Centennial (10% AA) (120 min.)	1.5 oz.	9 oz.
Mt. Hood (end of boil)	2 oz.	12 oz.

Barley Wine Specifications

Mash:	2 hours at 152 °F (67 °C) dropping to 147 °F (64 °C)
Boil:	2 hours
IBUs:	Low
OG:	25 °Plato
TG:	5 °Plato
ABV:	10.5%
Ferment Temp.:	70 °F (21 °C)
Yeast:	English ale
Ferment Time:	2 weeks
Aging (prior to packaging):	2–3 months

Rob's "Big 12" Barley Wine

Brewers: Rob Moline and Steve Zimmerman

Malt	5 Gallons	1 Barrel
Schreier two-row pale malt	15.5 lb.	93 lb.
DWC pale malt	1.2 lb.	7 lb.
Schreier caramel malt (30 °L)	4.75 lb.	28.5 lb.

Hops	5 Gallons	1 Barrel
Galena (11.2% AA) (60 min.)	1.6 oz.	9 oz.
Cascade (5.5% AA) (60 min.)	2 oz.	11.5 oz.
Willamette (4.7% AA)		
(end of boil)	2 oz.	11.5 oz.

Barley Wine Specifications

Mash:	90 minutes at 152 °F (67 °C)
Boil:	1.5 hours
IBUs:	63
OG:	1.096 (24 °P)
TG:	1.016 (4 °P)
ABV:	10.4%
Ferment Temp.:	68 °F (20 °C)
Yeast:	Lallemand dry Nottingham English ale plus Lallemand dry EC-1118 Champagne yeast added at the end of ale yeast fermentation
Ferment Time:	1–2 weeks
Aging (prior to packaging):	minimum of 4 months

Note: This recipe is based on Litte Apple Brewing Company's "Big 12" Barley Wine, winner of the gold medal in the barley wine category at the 1996 GABF.

Festivals

There are actually now a number of beer festivals in the United States that showcase barley wine—a good example of the renewed interest in the style. The West Coast has several with that bent, but the first of its kind (that we know of) was done on the East Coast at the Brickskeller in Washington, D.C.

The Brickskeller's owner, Maurice Coja, has been putting on beer events and tastings for over twelve years. The Brickskeller had its first barley wine tastings in 1990 and the event has been growing in popularity every year since. The Brickskeller is truly a unique place—it focuses on beer sampling, not beer drinking. Maurice wants to surprise your palate. He focuses on beer (and ethnic American food) as an art form and encourages people to try something different. He brings in food from all over the country: buffalo steaks from the Dakotas, piroshkis from a small

Polish neighborhood in Philadelphia, Kalua Pig from the Pueo Poi Factory just outside of Hilo, Hawaii (served with Taro chips, ulu, and Kulolo . . . *so ono bra, broke da mouth*). Maurice also has over 850 bottled beer selections to choose from. He only has draft beer when there's some left over from a recent tasting. Despite no regular draft beers, he has spent several thousands of dollars on a state-of-the-art refrigeration system that has three separate temperature-controlled areas to accommodate every kind of beer style. Maurice

Owner David Keene of the Toronado, where the Toronado Barley Wine Festival is held every February.

goes to (what some would call) excessive lengths to get special and unusual beers into his place. You never know what you'll find there. If you are anywhere near D.C., it is well worth a visit. The Brickseller's address is 1523 22nd N.W., Washington, D.C., and their phone number is (202) 293-1885.

The West Coast ground breaker was The Toronado's barley wine festival in San Francisco. It is the biggest in terms of the number of barley wines to taste and probably the smallest in number of attendees. The Toronado, with its impressive array of both draft and bottled products, has long been a destination for beer lovers from around the country. Proprietor David Keene is a true beer aficionado. For his week-long "festival," he rounds up barley wines from all over the West Coast and a few from other regions. The 1997 festival featured fifty-one barley wines, all on draft. The effort that goes into fitting that many kegs into his cooler is truly amazing—it requires that he take all of his regular draft beers off tap for that week. Many of the barley wines featured are consecutive years from the same breweries, including three different vintages of Bigfoot! If by chance you blaze through all the barley wines, you can start to work on David's regular line-up of bottled Belgian beers or maybe the cask conditioned ales. The Toranado's address is 547 Haight St., San Francisco, California, and their phone number is (415) 863-2267. While in San Francisco check out a few other good beer places: Zeitgeist Motorcycle Club, Lucky 13, Twenty Tank Brewery, and The Beach Chalet.

In the last few years Anchorage, Alaska, has really become quite the beer town. It is home to several good breweries and a few great watering holes. The Rail Yard, Bird Creek, Cusac's, Denali, Glacier, Midnight Sun, and Sleeping Lady breweries are all right there. These breweries are putting out some nice, well-made beers.

In 1996, two Anchorage publicans, Bill Opinsky and Maurice MacDonald (owners of Humpy's and O'Brady's, respectively), formed Beer Bellies, Inc., and embarked on a mission to put together the first Great Alaskan Winter Brew and Barley Wine Festival. This event (held in February) is larger in scope than the other two and features a wide variety of beers. The beers come from around the country and from around the world. The event focuses on, but not exclusively, winter brews and barley wines. At the second Great Alaskan Winter Brew and Barley Wine Festival, there were over 225 beers to try of which 35 were barley wines and 25 winter seasonals. The beer festival is held in conjunction with Fur Rondez-vous (*sic*), Anchorage's version of Mardi Gras. (It's actually much colder than Mardi Gras, but has the distinct advantage of being infinitely more civilized, even though it is up there in the land of bush pilots and moose juice.)

The weather is rather conducive to drinking a good strong beer, if for no other reason than to ward off frostbite. All the Fur Rondez-vous events surrounding this well-run beer festival make for an especially good time. If you do make it up there during that week, make sure to see the amazing outdoor ice sculpting contest. There are also a good many places worth checking out, including Humpy's, Chilcot Charlie's, O'Brady's, Railway Brewing Company, Glacier Brewhouse, Cusac's, and the Snow Goose Brewery.

Troubleshooting

Question: What do I do if my fermentation stops at 13 °Plato (1.052)?

The first thing is to try to establish why the fermentation stopped. First check to see if the beer is too cold; if so, warm it up to 70 °F (21 °C). If it was too cold, the yeast has probably fallen out of suspension. If the yeast has fallen out of suspension (either from cooling down or otherwise), you will need to rouse the yeast. This can be done a number of ways at home or with an open fermenter. If you have a closed fermenter, you can blow CO_2 in through the bottom to lift the yeast off the bottom and get it back into suspension.

If the beer is warm enough and there is yeast in suspension, then the next question to answer is whether there was enough oxygen in the wort to get the fermentation started. If there was not, or if you don't know, or if the yeast has not responded to rousing and warming, then you may need to add more oxygen to the fermenter. I know this sounds mad, but what other choices are left? To package it at 13 °Plato? This is a "what do you have to lose option." With a gravity this high, you are bound to get some fermentation that will use up any oxygen that you put in and the CO_2 production of fermentation will scrub

off any left over. We promise. We have done it before.

And if you still are not fermenting in 12 to 24 hours, maybe the alcohol level is too high for the yeast strain that you used. It might be helpful to add new or a different (more alcohol tolerant) strain of yeast from a recent fermentation. If you do repitch more yeast, make sure to give it a good amount of oxygen to really get it going. It will quickly use up the oxygen in solution and get you on your fermenting way.

Question: I didn't follow your excellent advice and now I have set my mash bed. What do I do?

A stuck, set, or compressed mash is a fairly common occurrence

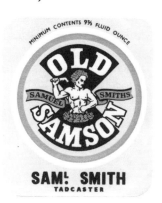

when making high-gravity all-grain beers. Because there is so much grain in the lauter tun, the weight of the mash bed pushing down on the plates (or screens) can clog the open spaces in the screens. This will reduce your throughput of wort to a trickle. Never a good thing. There are several ways to correct this problem.

One way is to underlet the mash bed or force hot water up from the bottom of the lauter vessel (under the screens). This may lift the mash bed off of the screens enough to allow you to continue with the runoff. This is the simplest and fastest of your options. But it has the disadvantage of diluting the wort you are running into the kettle, reducing the overall gravity of your brew.

A second solution to fixing a set mash bed is to stop the runoff and stir the whole mash bed up again, making sure that you really stir all the way down to the screens. This will not reduce your gravity but it will be more difficult and take longer because, after stirring the mash, you will have to recirculate the wort until it runs bright again. Another downside is all that stirring, if not done gently, could aerate the wort. Hot-side aeration is a bad thing.

A third way is to leave it alone and suffer through a protracted runoff that may take several hours. This is often the best option if you have a lot of spare time. Of course this may not be an option with some brews where the mash bed sets down so hard that it actually stops the flow of wort through the screens. Then you *must* choose another option.

And fourth, totally avoid these scenarios by (1) having a lot of luck, (2) not recirculating or running off too fast (thus setting the bed), (3) being gentle and slow (something most men are not very good at), (4) not overcrushing your grain, or (5) not using excessive amounts of dark malt or wheat in your high-gravity beers.

Question: I just stopped my runoff but it is still at 12 °Plato. Should I dump it down the drain?

No, you don't have to. Sending it down the drain would be very wasteful. Plus a wort of that gravity has a high BOD (biochemical oxygen demand) and your local sewer municipality would fine you if they caught you sending it down the drain in any real quantity. You can use that wort to make a "small beer." This a traditional brewing practice that dates back thousands of years. It gives you a free mild beer out of the deal. The last small beer I made was actually better than the barley wine that preceded it.

Question: I am sure that I put in too much hops. My month-old barley wine tastes like a Sweet Tart™. What can I do to save it?

If your barley wine is too hoppy, let it age. Even the

most bitter beer will mellow in three or four years. Aging can change beers in many ways, some of them beneficial. Besides, it has got to be better than putting it down the drain.

Your other option is blending. If it really is too hoppy or you have already waited two or three years, you do have the option of blending it off with a less hoppy beer. But this could have the drawback of just creating twice as much not-so-tasty beer.

Question: I just finished runoff, the kettle is full, and my gravity reading is 10 °Plato low. Am I doomed to have a wimpy barley wine?

No. Just boil for a bit longer than you had planned to. If you are getting a good evaporation rate, an extra 30 to 60 minutes of boiling can make a real difference in your original gravity. Just remember only boil for 90 minutes or less with the hops and we recommend that you don't exceed 3 or 3 1/2 hours of total boiling time. This is one reason it is good to take periodic gravity readings from the kettle throughout the boil. That way, you will know if extra boiling is going to be needed before you add the hops.

Question: My barley wine is cloudy. What can I do to make it bright and clear?

We recommend you give it another three to six months of cold aging (at or below 52 °F [11 °C]). If that doesn't work, then there is isinglass, clarigen finings, or filtration. But, be warned, filtering a beer always seems to remove some of the things that you liked in the beer along with the things you wanted to get rid of. That's why cold aging for months on end is usually the best option.

Question: I bottle-conditioned my barley wine. I put it in the bottle at a specific gravity of 1.020 (5 °Plato) and when I opened the first bottle three weeks later, it was flat. What can I do?

First, be glad that you don't have gushing overcarbonated bottles that will explode in the basement next month. Second, wait another month and see if you do get some carbonation to build up. Often high-gravity beer doesn't do so well bottle conditioning. Sometimes it can take months to get the correct amount of carbonation. Some people don't even prime bottle-conditioned barley wines and rely on that last bit of slow fermentation to give the beer the condition desired (but that is tricky and you really have to know your yeast to pull that off). And third, you may have to open each bottle and dose in a small amount of an alcohol-tolerant yeast. You can do this by adding a tiny bit from a previous fermentation or by adding a small grain of dried yeast to each bottle. We prefer the latter. But whenever you add extra yeast, be fanatically sanitary because you don't want to introduce any other microorganisms.

Question: My significant other hates the smell of my homebrewing and is threatening to leave me if I don't clean up my act.

As we see it you have four realistic options: (1) Leave them. It would never have worked out anyway. (2) Brew when your partner isn't home and then blame the smell on the local micobrewery. (3) Spend a huge amount of money from your joint bank account on building an outbuilding to brew in. This option lets you get all those techno-geek things that you always wanted (like plumbed natural gas or a temperature-controlled fermentation room) for half the price. (4) Brew in the great outdoors. (Don't laugh, we have friends who do just that!)

U.S. and Canadian Barley Wine Breweries

United States

Appleton Brewing Co./Adler Brau
Bucky Red (10.0% ABV)
Assets Grille/Southwest Brewing Co.
Ol' Avalanche Barley Wine (7.5% ABW)
Atlantic Coast Brewing Ltd.
Santi-Freeze (11.4% ABV)
Bardo Rodeo
White Lightning (9.5% ABV)
Big Time Brewing Co.
Old Wooly (6.2% ABV)
Birkebeiner Brewing Co.
Ol' Grungy Bastard (13.0% ABV)
Blind Pig Brewing Co.
Old Blue Granite Barley Wine (9.3% ABV)
Bloomington Brewing Co./One World Enterprises
Old Bobby (8.5% ABV)
Bluegrass Brewing Co.
BBL Barley Wine (7.3% ABV)

Boardwalk Bistro
Barley Wine (11.0% ABV)
Boston Beer Works
Hercules Strong Ale (10.0% ABV)
BridgePort Brewing Co.
BridgePort Old Knucklehead
Brimstone Brewing Co.
Big Strong Ale (13.5% ABV)
Broad Ripple Brewing Co.
Limping Malard (8.5% ABV)
Broad Ripple Brewing Co.
Wee Ale Heavy
Butterfield Brewing Co.
Anniversary Barleywine
Cafe on the Square and Brewpub
Christmas Ale (10.0% ABV)
Carver Brewing Co.
Big Grizz Barley Wine (9.0% ABW)
Cascade Lakes Brewing Co.
Old Curmudgeon (10.0% ABW)
CooperSmith's Pub and Brewing
Black Powder Barley Wine (8.0% ABW)
Dock Steet Brewing Co. Brewery and Restaurant
Barley Wine
Dock Street Brewery and Restaurant (No. 2)
Barley Wine
El Toro Brewing Co.
Kick Ace
Elysian Brewing Co.
Cyclops (Old One Eye) (10% ABV)
Eske's Brew Pub/Sangre de Cristo Brewing Co.
Bert and Ernie Barley Wine (8.5% ABV)
Eugene City Brewing Co./West Brothers Bar-B-Q
Old Curmudgeon Barley Wine (6.5% ABW)

Faultline Brewing Co. Inc.
Faultline Barley Wine
Fish Brewing Co./Fishbowl Pub
Leviathan Barley Wine (8.0% ABV)
Flat Branch Brewing Co.
Old Cave Dweller (7.6% ABV)
Flying Dog Brewpub
Blitzen's Gnarly Barley Wine (8.9% ABV)
Full Sail Brewpub and Tasting Room
Full Sail Barley Wine
Golden City Brewery
Centurion Barley Wine (10.0% ABV)
Goose Island Brewing Co.
Old Abernation Barley Wine (11.5% ABV)
Goose Island Brewing Co.
Winter Warmer (9.0% ABV)
Great Dane Pub and Brewing Co.
Barleywine (7.2% ABW)
Grizzly Bay Brewing Co.
Smokin' Hole Barley Wine (8.5% ABV)
Hart Brewing Co. Inc.
Snow Cap Ale (7.0% ABV)
Hops Bistro and Brewery (No. 1)
Barley Wine (10.0% ABV)
Hubcap Brewery and Kitchen
Ozone Ale (9.5% ABV)
Humboldt Brewery
Cheshire Cat (10.0% ABV)
Humes Brewing Co. Inc.
Organic Barleywine-Style Ale (9.4% ABW)
Joe's Brewing Co.
Joe's Barleywine (9.8% ABV)
Lafayette Brewing Co.
Big Boris (8.5% ABV)

Barley Wine

Mad River Brewing Co.
John Barleycorn Barley Wine (8.0% ABW)
Marin Brewing Co.
Old Dipsea Barley Wine (9.0% ABV)
McGuire's Irish Pub and Brewery
"What the Gentleman on the Floor Is Having" (9.5% ABV)
McNeill's Brewery
Bucksnort Barley Wine (8.0% ABV)
Mishawaka Brewing Co.
Resolution Ale (8.0% ABV)
Murphys Creek Brewing Co.
Deliverance (9.3% ABW)
Napa Valley Brewing Co.
Calistoga Ole Water Tower Barley Wine (7.0% ABW)
Old Dominion Brewing Co.
Dominion Millennium (10.4% ABV)
Pacific Coast Brewing Co.
Code Blue Barley Wine (9.0% ABV)
Pacific Hop Exchange
Barbary Coast Barley Wine (11.5% ABV)
Pike Brewing Co.
Old Bawdy Barley Wine (9.9% ABV)
Pizza Port/Solana Beach Brewery
Old Boneyard's Barley Wine (10.8% ABV)
Prescott Brewing Co.
Big Butte Barley Wine (8.4% ABW)
Quality Assured Brewing
Belle Dock Barley Wine
Richbrau Brewing Co.
John Barleycorn's Barleywine (12.5% ABV)
Richbrau Brewing Co.
Tell Tale Ale (8.4% ABV)
Rio Bravo Restaurant & Brewery
Big Bob's Barley Wine (8.7% ABV)

Rock Bottom Brewery (No. 2)
Ol' Thumper Barley Wine (8.5% ABV)
Rogue Ales/Oregon Brewing Co.
Old Crustacean Barley Wine
Rubicon Brewing Co.
Blonde Barley Wine (9.5% ABV)
Saint Louis Brewery/Schlafly Brands
Old Possum Barley Wine (8.0% ABV)
San Francisco Brewing Co.
Oofty Goofty (9.0% ABV)
Santa Cruz Brewing Co. and Front Street Pub
Pacific Beacon (8.0% ABW)
Santa Fe Brewing Co.
Chicken Killer Barley Wine (8.0% ABW)
Santa Rosa Brewing Co.
Old Winkie
Seabright Brewery Inc.
Barley Wine Style Ale (9.0% ABV)
Seattle Brewers
Beache's Brew (10.0% ABV)
Shipyard Brewing Co.
Prelude Ale (7.3% ABV)
Sierra Nevada Brewing Co.
Sierra Nevada Bigfoot Barleywine-Style Ale (8.0% ABW)
Sonoma Brewing Co.
Big River Barleywine (8.5% ABV)
Sonoma Brewing Co.
Noche Buena Barley Wine (9.0% ABV)
Spanish Peaks Brewery
Big Dog Barley Wine (9.5% ABV)
Spanish Peaks Brewing Co.
Wee Nip Barley Wine Ale (9.5% ABV)
St. Stan's Brewery/Pub and Restaurant
Barley Wine (7.5% ABV)

Barley Wine

Sunday River Brewing Co.
Brass Balls Barleywine (9.0% ABV)
Sutter Brewing Co. Inc.
Jackass XX Stout (11.0% ABV)
Traffic Jam and Snug
T. J. Barley Wine (8.0% ABV)
Trinity Beer Works Inc.
Winter Warmer (9.0% ABV)
Troy Brewing Co.
St. Nick's Nectar (10.0% ABV)
Twenty Tank Brewery
Nyack Barley Wine (8.0% ABW)
TwoRows Restaurant and Brewery
Blackbeard's Barley Wine
Umpqua Brewing Co.
Double Red Barley Wine (7.8% ABV)
Walnut Brewery
Old Thumper (8.5% ABW)
Weinkeller Brewpub (No. 2)
Piccadilly Barley Wine (7.5% ABV)
Wild Duck Brewery and Restaurant
Duckblind Barleywine (10.0% ABV)
Wild River Brewing and Pizza Co.
Wild River Cave Bear Barley Wine (8.0% ABW)
Wild River Brewing and Pizza Co. (No. 2)
Cave Bear Barley Wine (8.0% ABW)
Wynkoop Brewing Co.
Emma's Barleywine (7.0% ABW)
Wynkoop Brewing Co.
Holiday Ale (6.5% ABW)

Canada

Alley Kat Brewing Co.
Olde Deuteronomy (8.0% ABV)
Brewsters Brewing Co. and Restaurant (No. 2)
Blue Monk Barley Wine (7.5% ABV)
Brewsters Brewing Co. and Restaurant/Cornerstone Inn (No. 3)
Barley Wine (7.5% ABV)
Brewsters Brewing Co. and Restaurant/Cornerstone Inn (No. 3)
Blue Monk Barley Wine (7.5% ABV)
B. Hwakker Brewing Co. Ltd.
Missiletow Ale/Cyclone Barley Wine (8.9% ABV)
Glatt Bros Brewing Co.
Fallen Angel Barley Wine (7.0% ABV)
Shaftebury Brewing Co. Ltd.
S'bury Celebration 100 X-Mas (8.8% ABV)

Unit Conversion Chart

Index	lb. to kg	oz. to g	fl. oz. to ml	gal. to l US	gal. to l UK
0.25	0.11	7	7	0.95	1.14
0.50	0.23	14	15	1.89	2.27
0.75	0.34	21	22	2.84	3.41
1.00	0.45	28	30	3.79	4.55
1.25	0.57	35	37	4.73	5.68
1.50	0.68	43	44	5.68	6.82
1.75	0.79	50	52	6.62	7.96
2.00	0.91	57	59	7.57	9.09
2.25	1.02	64	67	8.52	10.23
2.50	1.13	71	74	9.46	11.36
2.75	1.25	78	81	10.41	12.50
3.00	1.36	85	89	11.36	13.64
3.25	1.47	92	96	12.30	14.77
3.50	1.59	99	103	13.25	15.91
3.75	1.70	106	111	14.19	17.05
4.00	1.81	113	118	15.14	18.18
4.25	1.93	120	126	16.09	19.32
4.50	2.04	128	133	17.03	20.46
4.75	2.15	135	140	17.98	21.59
5.00	2.27	142	148	18.93	22.73
5.25	2.38	149	155	19.87	23.87
5.50	2.49	156	163	20.82	25.00
5.75	2.61	163	170	21.77	26.14
6.00	2.72	170	177	22.71	27.28
6.25	2.84	177	185	23.66	28.41
6.50	2.95	184	192	24.60	29.55
6.75	3.06	191	200	25.55	30.69
7.00	3.18	198	207	26.50	31.82
7.25	3.29	206	214	27.44	32.96
7.50	3.40	213	222	28.39	34.09
7.75	3.52	220	229	29.34	35.23
8.00	3.63	227	237	30.28	36.37
8.25	3.74	234	244	31.23	37.50
8.50	3.86	241	251	32.18	38.64
8.75	3.97	248	259	33.12	39.78
9.00	4.08	255	266	34.07	40.91
9.25	4.20	262	274	35.01	42.05
9.50	4.31	269	281	36.96	43.19
9.75	4.42	276	288	37.91	44.32
10.00	4.54	283	296	37.85	45.46
10.25	4.65	291	303	38.80	46.60
10.50	4.76	298	310	39.75	47.73
10.75	4.88	305	318	40.69	48.87
11.00	4.99	312	325	41.64	50.01
11.25	5.10	319	333	42.58	51.14
11.50	5.22	326	340	43.53	52.28
11.75	5.33	333	347	44.48	53.41
12.00	5.44	340	355	45.42	54.55

By Philip W. Fleming and Joachim Schüring.   Reprinted with permission from Zymurgy®.

| qt. to l | | pt. to l | | tsp. | tbsp. | cup |
US	UK	US	UK	to ml	to ml	to ml
0.24	0.28	0.12	0.14	1.2	3.7	59
0.47	0.57	0.24	0.28	2.5	7.4	118
0.71	0.85	0.35	0.43	3.7	11.1	177
0.95	1.14	0.47	0.57	4.9	14.8	237
1.18	1.42	0.59	0.71	6.2	18.5	296
1.42	1.70	0.71	0.85	7.4	22.2	355
1.66	1.99	0.83	0.99	8.6	25.9	414
1.89	2.27	0.95	1.14	9.9	29.6	473
2.13	2.56	1.06	1.28	11.1	33.3	532
2.37	2.84	1.18	1.42	12.3	37.0	591
2.60	3.13	1.30	1.56	13.6	40.2	651
2.84	3.41	1.42	1.70	14.8	44.4	710
3.08	3.69	1.54	1.85	16.0	48.1	769
3.31	3.98	1.66	1.99	17.3	51.8	828
3.55	4.26	1.77	2.13	18.5	55.4	887
3.79	4.55	1.89	2.27	19.7	59.1	946
4.02	4.83	2.01	2.42	20.9	62.8	1,005
4.26	5.11	2.13	2.56	22.2	66.5	1,065
4.50	5.40	2.25	2.70	23.4	70.2	1,124
4.73	5.68	2.37	2.84	24.6	73.9	1,183
4.97	5.97	2.48	2.98	25.9	77.6	1,242
5.20	6.25	2.60	3.13	27.1	81.3	1,301
5.44	6.53	2.72	3.27	28.3	85.0	1,360
5.68	6.82	2.84	3.41	29.6	88.7	1,419
5.91	7.10	2.96	3.55	30.8	92.4	1,479
6.15	7.39	3.08	3.69	32.0	96.1	1,538
6.39	7.67	3.19	3.84	33.3	99.8	1,597
6.62	7.96	3.31	3.98	34.5	103.5	1,656
6.86	8.24	3.43	4.12	35.7	107.2	1,715
7.10	8.52	3.55	4.26	37.0	110.9	1,774
7.33	8.81	3.67	4.40	38.2	114.6	1,834
7.57	9.09	3.79	4.55	39.4	118.3	1,893
7.81	9.38	3.90	4.69	40.7	122.0	1,952
8.04	9.66	4.02	4.83	41.9	125.7	2,011
8.28	9.94	4.14	4.97	43.1	129.4	2,070
8.52	10.23	4.26	5.11	44.4	133.1	2,129
8.75	10.51	4.38	5.26	45.6	136.8	2,188
9.99	10.80	4.50	5.40	46.8	140.5	2,248
9.23	11.08	4.61	5.54	48.1	144.2	2,307
9.46	11.36	4.73	5.68	49.3	147.9	2,366
9.70	11.65	4.85	5.82	50.5	151.6	2,425
9.94	11.93	4.97	5.97	51.8	155.3	2,484
10.17	12.22	5.09	6.11	53.0	159.0	2,543
10.41	12.50	5.20	6.25	54.2	162.6	2,602
10.65	12.79	5.32	6.39	55.4	166.3	2,662
10.88	13.07	5.44	6.53	56.7	170.0	2,721
11.12	13.35	5.56	6.68	57.9	173.7	2,780
11.36	13.64	5.68	6.82	59.1	177.4	2,839

Glossary

acrospire. The germinal plant-growth of the barley kernel.

ad-humulone. The third (or sometimes second) most prevalent of the three alpha acids, which, when isomerized during boiling of the wort, provides most of the bittering characteristic that comes from hops.

adjunct. Any unmalted grain or other fermentable ingredient added to the mash.

adjuncts. Sources of fermentable extract other than malted barley. Principally corn, rice, wheat, unmalted barley, and glucose (dextrose).

aerate. To force atmospheric air or oxygen into solution. Introducing air to the wort at various stages of the brewing process.

aeration. The action of introducing air to the wort at various stages of the brewing process.

aerobic. In the presence of or requiring oxygen.

agar (Agar-agar). A non-nitrogenous, gelatinous solidifying agent, more heat-stable than gelatin. A culture medium for microbial analysis.

agglutination. The grouping of cells by adhesion.

airlock. See *fermentation lock.*

airspace. See *ullage.*

albumin. Intermediate soluble protein subject to coagulation upon heating. Hydrolyzed to peptides and amino acids by proteolytic enzymes.

alcohol by volume (ABV). The percentage of volume of alcohol per volume of beer. To calculate the approximate volumetric alcohol content, subtract the final gravity from the original gravity and divide the result by 75. For example: $1.050 - 1.012 = .038 / 0.0075 = 5\%$ ABV.

alcohol by weight (ABW). The percentage weight of alcohol per volume of beer. For example: 3.2% alcohol by weight = 3.2 grams of alcohol per 100 centiliters of beer. Alcohol by weight can be converted to alcohol by volume by multiplying by 0.795.

aldehyde. An organic compound that is a precursor to ethanol in a normal beer fermentation via the EMP pathway. In the presence of excess air, this reaction can be reversed, with alcohols being oxidized to very complex, unpleasant-tasting aldehydes, typically papery/cardboardy/sherry notes. These compounds are characterized as oxidized alcohols, with a terminal CHO group.

ale. 1. Historically, an unhopped malt beverage. 2. Now a generic term for hopped beers produced by top fermentation, as opposed to lagers, which are produced by bottom fermentation.

aleurone layer. The enzyme- and pentosan-bearing layer enveloping, and inseparable from, the malt endosperm.

all-extract beer. A beer made with only malt extract as opposed to one made from barley, or a combination of malt extract and barley.

all-grain beer. A beer made with only malted barley as opposed to one made from malt extract, or from malt extract and malted barley.

alpha acid unit (AAU). The number of AAUs in a hop addition is equal to the weight of the addition in ounces times the alpha acid percentage. Thus 1 ounce of 5% alpha acid hops contain 5 AAUs. AAU is the same as HBU.

alpha acid (a-acid). The principle source of bitterness from hops when isomerized by boiling. These separate but related alpha acids come from the soft alpha resin of the hop.

alpha acid. A soft resin in hop cones. When boiled, alpha acids are converted to iso-alpha-acids.

alt. The German word for old. This is a top-fermenting style of beer that undergoes a cold lagering for maturation.

ambient temperature. The surrounding temperature.

amino acids. The building blocks of proteins. Essential components of wort, required for adequate yeast growth. They are the smallest product of protein cleavage; simple nitrogenous matter.

amylodextrin. From the diastatic reduction of starch; a-limit dextrin; the most complex dextrin from hydrolysis of starch with diastase. Mahogany (red-brown) color reaction with iodine.

amylolysis. The enzymatic reduction of starch to soluble fractions.

amylopectin. Branched starch chain; shell and paste-forming starch. Unable to be entirely saccharified by amylolytic enzymes, a-limit dextrins, or amylodextrins, remain.

amylose. Straight chain of native starch; a-D-glucose (glucose dehydrate) molecules joined by a-(1-4) links. Gives deep blue-black color with iodine.

anaerobic. Conditions under which there is not enough oxygen for respiratory metabolic function. Anaerobic microorganisms are those that can function without the presence of free molecular oxygen.

analyte. A chemical compound that is the target of a particular assay or test system.

anion. An electronegative ion.

apparent attenuation. A simple measure of the extent of fermentation that a wort has undergone in the process of becoming beer. Using gravity units (GU), Balling (B), or Plato (P) units to express gravity, apparent attenuation is equal to the original gravity minus the terminal gravity divided by the original gravity. The result is expressed as a percentage and equals 65% to 80% for most beers.

apparent extract. A term used to indicate the terminal gravity of a beer.

aqueous. Of water.

ash. The residue left behind after all the organic matter of a substance has been incinerated. It consists of mineral matter and serves as a measure of the inorganic salts that were in the original substance.

attemper. To regulate or modify the temperature.

attenuate. Reduction of the extract/density by yeast metabolism.

attenuation. The reduction in the wort's specific gravity caused by the transformation of sugars into alcohol and carbon-dioxide gas.

autolysis. Yeast death due to shock or nutrient-depleted solutions.

bacteriostatic. Bacteria-inhibiting.

Balling. A saccharometer invented by Carl Joseph Napoleon Balling in 1843, it is a standard for the measurement of the density of solutions. It is calibrated for 63.5 °F (17.5 °C), and graduated in grams per hundred, giving a direct reading of the percentage of extract by weight per 100 grams solution. For example: 10 °B = 10 grams of sugar per 100 grams of wort.

beerstone. Brownish gray mineral-like deposits left on fermentation equipment. Composed of calcium oxalate and organic residues.

blow-by (blow-off). A single-stage homebrewing fermentation method in which a plastic tube is fitted into the mouth of a carboy, with the other end submerged in a pail of sterile water. Unwanted residues and carbon dioxide are expelled through the tube, while air is prevented from coming into contact with the fermenting beer, thus avoiding contamination.

body. A qualitative indicator of the fullness or mouthfeel of a beer. Related to the proportion of unfermentable long-chain sugars or dextrins present in the beer.

Brettanomyces. A genus of yeasts that have a role in the production of some beers, such as modern *lambics* and Berliner *weisse* and historical porters.

brewer's gravity (SG). See *gravity.*

BU:GU ratio. The ratio of bitterness units to gravity units for a specific beer or group of beers. International bitterness units (IBU) are used for bitterness, and gravity units (GU) are used for the gravity component. For most beers and beer styles, the resulting ratio has a value between 0.3 and 1.0.

buffer. A substance capable of resisting changes in the pH of a solution.

calandria. A shrouded percolator for boiling wort. It can be internal or housed externally and fed by pipes with the use of pumps.

carbonates. Alkaline salts whose anions are derived from carbonic acid.

carbonation. The process of introducing carbon-dioxide gas into a liquid by: (1) injecting the finished beer with carbon dioxide; (2) adding young fermenting beer to finished beer for a renewed fermentation (kraeusening); (3) priming (adding sugar) to fermented wort prior to bottling, creating a secondary fermentation in the bottle; or (4) finishing fermentation under pressure.

carboy. A large glass, plastic, or earthenware bottle.

caryophylline. A secondary component of hop oil found in varying proportions in different varieties of hops.

cation. Electropositive ion.

cellulose. A polymer of sugar molecules that plays a structural rather than storage role. The sugars that make up cellulose cannot be liberated by the enzymes found in most plant systems.

chill haze. Haziness caused by protein and tannin during the secondary fermentation.

chill-proof. Cold conditioning to precipitate chill haze.

clarigen finings. Carrageen-based finings.

closed fermentation. Fermentation under closed, anaerobic conditions to minimize risk of contamination and oxidation.

co-humulone. The second (or sometimes third) most prevalent of the three alpha acids, which, when isomerized during boiling of the wort, provide most of the bittering characteristic that comes from hops.

coliform. Waterborne bacteria, often associated with pollution.

colloid. A gelatinous substance in solution.

decoction. Boiling, the part of the mash that is boiled.

density. The measurement of the weight of a solution, as compared with the weight of an equal volume of pure water.

dextrin. Soluble polysaccharide fraction from hydrolysis of starch by heat, acid, or enzyme.

diacetyl. See *diketone*.

diacetyl rest. A warm (55 to 70 °F [13 to 21 °C] rest which occurs during fermentation. During the diacetyl rest yeast metabolize diacetyl and other byproducts of fermentation.

diastase. Starch-reducing enzymes; usually alpha- and beta-amylase, but also limit dextrinase and a-glucosidase (maltase).

diastatic malt extract. A type of malt extract containing the diastatic enzymes naturally found in malt and needed for conversion of starch into sugar. This type of extract is sometimes used in recipes that contain grain adjuncts such as corn or rice.

diketone. A class of aromatic, volatile compounds perceivable in minute concentration, from yeast or *Pediococcus* bacteria metabolism. Most significantly the butter aroma of diacetyl, a vicinal diketone (VDK). The other significant compound relevant to brewing is 2,3-pentanedione.

dimethyl sulfide (DMS). An important sulfur-carrying compound originating in malt. Adds a crisp, "lager-like" character at low levels, and corn or cabbage flavors at high levels.

disaccharides. Sugar group; two monosaccharide molecules joined by the removal of a water molecule.

dry hopping. The addition of hops to the primary fermenter, the secondary fermenter, or to casked beer to add aroma and hop character to the finished beer without adding significant bitterness.

dry malt. Malt extract in powdered form.

EBC (European Brewery Convention). See *SRM.*

enzymes. Protein-based organic catalysts that affect changes in the compositions of the substances they act upon.

erythrodextrin. Tasteless intermediate dextrin. Large a-limit dextrins. Faint red reaction with iodine.

essential oil. The aromatic volatile compounds from the hop.

ester. A class of organic compounds created from the reaction of an alcohol and an organic acid. These tend to have fruity aromas and are detectable at low concentrations.

esters. "Ethereal salts" such as ethyl acetate; aromatic compounds from fermentation composed of an acid and an alcohol, such as the "banana" ester. Formed by yeast enzymes from an alcohol and an acid. Associated with ale and high-temperature fermentations, esters also arise to some extent with pure lager yeast cultures, though more so with low wort oxygenation, high initial fermentation temperatures, and high-gravity wort. Top-fermenting yeast strains are prized for their ability to produce particular mixes of esters.

extract. The amount of dissolved materials in the wort after mashing and lautering malted barley and/or malt adjuncts such as corn and rice.

extraction. Drawing out the soluble essence of the malt or hops.

farnescene. A secondary component of hop oil found in varying proportions in different varieties of hops.

fecal bacteria. Coliform bacteria associated with sewage.

fermentation lock. A one-way valve that allows carbon dioxide gas to escape from the fermenter while excluding contaminants.

final specific gravity. The specific gravity of a beer when fermentation is complete.

fining. (n.) A clarifying agent. (v.) The process of adding clarifying agents to beer during secondary fermentation to precipitate suspended matter. Examples of clarifying agents are: isinglass, gelatin, bentonite, silica gel, or polyvinyl pyrrolidone.

flocculation. The tendency of yeast to clump together at the end of fermentation. The greater the tendency for the yeast to flocculate, the faster it will drop out of the solution, creating clearer or brighter beer.

germination. Sprouting of the barley kernel, to initiate enzyme development and conversion of the malt.

glucophilic. An organism that thrives on glucose.

gravity (SG). Specific gravity as expressed by brewers; specific gravity 1.046 is expressed as 1046. Density of a solution as compared to water; expressed in grams per milliliter (1 ml water weighs 1 g, hence sp gr 1.000 = SG 1000; sp gr 1.046 = SG 1046).

gravity units (GU). A form of expressing specific gravity in formulas as a whole number. It is equal to the significant digits to the right of the decimal point (1.055 SG becomes 55 GU and 1.108 SG becomes 108 GU).

green malt. Malt that has been steeped and germinated and is ready for kilning.

hemocytometer. A device used for counting blood cells (or brewers' yeast) under a microscope.

hexose. Sugar molecules of six carbon atoms. Includes glucose, fructose, lactose, mannose, and galactose.

homebrewers bittering units (HBU). A formula adopted by the American Homebrewers Association to measure bitterness of beer. Example: 1.5 ounces of hops at 10% alpha acid for 5 gallons: 1.5 × 10 = 15 HBU per 5 gallons. Same as AAU.

homofermentive. Organisms that metabolize only one specific carbon source.

hop pellets. Finely powdered hop cones compressed into tablets. Hop pellets are 20 to 30% more bitter by weight than the same hop variety in loose form. Hop pellets are less subject to alpha acid losses than are whole hops.

humulene. A primary component of the essential oil of the hop cone. Although rarely found in beer in this native form, it is processed into a number of flavor-active compounds that are significant in beer. The quantity of humulene found in a hop varies by variety, year, and growing region.

humulone. The most prevalent of the three alpha acids, which, when isomerized during boiling of the wort, provides most of the bittering characteristic that comes from hops.

hydrolysis. Decomposition of matter into soluble fractions by either acids or enzymes, in water.

hydrometer. A glass instrument used to measure the specific gravity of liquids as compared to water, consisting of a graduated stem resting on a weighted float.

hydroxide. A compound, usually alkaline, containing the OH (hydroxyl) group.

inoculate. The introduction of a microbe into surroundings capable of supporting its growth.

international bitterness unit (IBU). This is a standard unit that measures the concentration of iso-alpha acids in milligrams per liter (parts per million). Most procedures will also measure a small amount of uncharacterized soft resins, so IBUs are generally 5 to 15% higher than iso-alpha acid concentrations.

isinglass. A gelatinous substance made from the swim bladder of certain fish and added to beer as a fining agent.

isomer (iso). Organic compounds of identical composition and molecular weight, but having a different molecular structure.

kilning. The final stage in the malting of barley that prepares it for use by the brewer. Kilning reduces the moisture contained in the grain to approximately 4% and also roasts the malt to some extent. The degree of roasting affects the flavor and color of the malt as well as of the beer it produces.

kraeusen. (n.) The rocky head of foam which appears on the surface of the wort during fermentation. Also used to describe the period of fermentation characterized by a rich foam head. (v.) To add fermenting wort to fermented beer to induce carbonation through a secondary fermentation.

Lactobacillus. Species of bacteria that ferments wort sugars to produce lactic acid. Although considered undesirable in most breweries and beer styles, it plays a significant role in the production of some beers, such as Berliner *weisse* and *lambics.*

lactophilic. An organism that metabolizes lactate more readily than glucose.

lager. (n.) A generic term for any bottom-fermented beer. Lager brewing is now the predominant brewing method worldwide except in Britain where top-fermented ales dominate. (v.) To store beer at near-zero temperatures in order to precipitate yeast cells and proteins and improve taste.

lauter. The clear liquid of the mash after saccharification. The process of separating the clear liquid from the spent grain and husks.

lauter tun. A vessel in which the mash settles and the grains are removed from the sweet wort through a straining process. It has a false slotted bottom and spigot.

lipids. Fatlike substances, especially triacylglycerols and fatty acids. Negatively affect a beer's ability to form a foam head. Cause soapy flavors; when oxidized, contribute stale flavors.

liquefaction. The process by which alpha-amylase enzymes degrade soluble starch into dextrin.

malt. Barley that has been steeped in water, germinated, then dried in kilns. This process converts insoluble starches to soluble substances and sugars.

malt extract. A thick syrup or dry powder prepared from malt.

maltose. A disaccharide composed of two glucose molecules, and the primary sugar obtained by diastatic hydrolysis of starch. One-third the sweetness of sucrose.

mashing. Mixing ground malt with water to extract the fermentables, degrade haze-forming proteins, and convert grain starches to fermentable sugars and nonfermentable carbohydrates.

melanoidins. Color-producing compounds produced through a long series of chemical reactions that begin with the combination of a sugar and an amino acid.

methylene blue. A stain used to test the viability (ability to reproduce) of a yeast cell.

modification. 1. The physical and chemical changes that occur in barley during malting where complex molecules are broken down to simpler, soluble molecules. 2. The degree to which malt has undergone these changes, as determined by the growth of the acrospire. The greater the degree of modification the more readily available starch there is and the lower the protein level.

mole. A unit of measure for chemical compounds. The amount of a substance that has a weight in grams numerically equal to the molecular weight of the substance. Also gram-molecular weight.

myrcene. A primary component of the essential oil of the hop cone. Although rarely found in beer in this native form, it is processed into a number of flavor-active compounds that are significant in beer. The quantity of myrcene found in a hop varies by variety, year, and growing region.

original gravity. The specific gravity of wort previous to fermentation. A measure of the total amount of dissolved solids in wort.

oxidation. 1. The combining of oxygen with other molecules, oftentimes causing off-flavors, as with oxidized alcohols to form aldehydes. 2. A reaction in which the atoms in an element lose electrons and its valence is correspondingly increased (oxidation-reduction reaction).

parti-gyle. An arcane system of brewing in which the first runnings of wort are taken to make a high-gravity beer, and the grain is then remashed to create another brew. This can be done yet again to make a third brew, all from the same grains. There is usually no sparging involved when using the parti-gyle system. With the advent of more sophisticated equipment that allowed lautering and sparging the parti-gyle system of brewing lost favor around the end of the nineteenth century.

pectin. Vegetable/fruit substance. A chain of galacturonic acid that becomes gelatinous in the presence of sugars and acids.

pentosan. Pentose-based complex carbohydrates, especially gums.

pentose. Sugar molecules of five carbon atoms. Monosaccharides.

peptonizing. The action of proteolytic enzymes upon protein, successively yielding albumin/proteoses, peptides, and amino acids.

pH. A measure of acidity or alkalinity of a solution, usually on a scale of one to fourteen, where seven is neutral.

phenols. Aromatic hydroxyl precursors of tannins/polyphenols. "Phenolic" in beer describes medicinal flavors from tannins, bacterial growth, cleaning compounds, or plastics.

phosphate. A salt or ester of phosphoric acid.

pitching. Inoculating sterile wort with a vigorous yeast culture.

Plato, degrees. Commercial brewers' standard for the measurement of the density of solutions, expressed as the equivalent weight of cane sugar in solution (calibrated on grams of sucrose per 100 grams of solution). Like degrees Balling, but Plato's computations are more exact.

Plato saccharometer. A saccharometer that expresses specific gravity as extract weight in a 100-gram solution at 68 °F (20 °C). A revised, more accurate version of Balling, developed by Dr. Plato.

polymer. A compound molecule formed by the joining of many smaller identical units. For example, polyphenols from phenols, polypeptides from peptides.

polyphenol. Complexes of phenolic compounds involved in chill haze formation and oxidative staling.

polysaccharides. Carbohydrate complexes, able to be reduced to monosaccharides by hydrolysis.

ppm. Parts per million. Equal to milligrams per liter (mg/l). The measurement of particles of matter in solution.

precipitation. Separation of suspended matter by sedimentation.

precursor. The starting materials or inputs for a chemical reaction.

primary fermentation. The first stage of fermentation, during which most fermentable sugars are converted to ethyl alcohol and carbon dioxide.

priming. The act of adding priming sugar to a still (or flat) beer so that it may develop carbonation.

priming solution. A solution of sugar in water added to aged beer at bottling to induce fermentation (bottle conditioning).

priming sugar. A small amount of corn, malt, or cane sugar added to bulk beer prior to racking or at bottling, to induce a new fermentation and create carbonation.

protein. Generally amorphous and colloidal complex amino acid containing about 16% nitrogen with carbon, hydrogen, oxygen, and possibly sulfur, phosphorous, and iron. True protein has a molecular weight of 17,000 to 150,000; in beer, protein will have been largely decomposed to a molecular weight of 5,000 to 12,000 (albumin or proteoses), 400 to 1,500 (peptides), or amino acids. Protein as a haze fraction ranges from molecular weight 10,000 to 100,000 (average 30,000), and as the stabilizing component of foam, from 12,000 to 20,000.

proteolysis. The reduction of protein by proteolytic enzymes to fractions.

racking. The process of transferring beer from one container to another, especially into the final package (bottles, kegs, etc.).

reagent. A substance involved in a reaction that identifies the strength of the substance being measured.

real ale. A style of beer found primarily in England, where it has been championed by the consumer rights group called the Campaign for Real Ale (CAMRA). Generally defined as beers that have undergone a secondary fermentation in the container from which they are served and that are served without the application of carbon dioxide.

resin. Noncrystalline (amorphous) plant excretions.

rest. Mash rest. Holding the mash at a specific temperature to induce certain enzymatic changes.

ropy fermentation. Viscous gelatinous blobs, or "rope," from bacterial contamination.

rousing. Creating turbulence by agitation; mixing.

ruh beer. The nearly fermented beer, ready for lagering. Cold secondary fermentation.

runnings. The wort or sweet liquid that is collected during the lautering of the wet mash.

saccharification. The naturally occurring process in which malt starch is converted into fermentable sugars, primarily maltose. Also called mashing since saccharification occurs during the mash rest.

saccharometer. An instrument that determines the sugar concentration of a solution by measuring the specific gravity.

secondary fermentation. 1. The second, slower stage of fermentation, which, depending on the type of beer, lasts from a few weeks to many months. 2. A fermentation occurring in bottles or casks and initiated by priming or by adding yeast.

sparge. The even distribution or spray of hot water over the saccharified mash to rinse free the extract from the grist.

sparging. Spraying the spent grains in the mash with hot water to retrieve the remaining malt sugar. This is done at the end of the mashing (saccharification) process.

specific gravity. A measure of a substance's density as compared to that of water, which is given the value of 1.000 at 39.2 °F (4 °C). Specific gravity has no accompanying units, because it is expressed as a ratio. Specific gravity is the density of a solution, in grams per milliliter.

SRM (Standard Reference Method) and EBC (European Brewery Convention). Two different analytical methods of describing color developed by comparing color samples. Degrees SRM, approximately equivalent to degrees Lovibond, are used by the ASBC (American Society of Brewing Chemists), while degrees EBC are European units. The following equations show approximate conversions: (EBC) = 2.65 × (SRM) − 1.2; SRM = 0.377 × (EBC) + 0.46.

starch. A polymer of sugar molecules, starch is the chief form of energy storage for most plants. It is from starch that the relevant sugars for brewing are derived.

starter. A batch of fermenting yeast, added to the wort to initiate fermentation.

steeping. The initial processing step in malting, where the raw barley is soaked in water and periodically aerated to induce germination.

strike temperature. The initial (target) temperature of the water when the malted barley is added to it to create the mash.

substratum. The substance in or on which an organism grows.

tannin. Astringent polyphenolic compounds, capable of colliding with proteins and either precipitating or forming haze fractions. Oxidized polyphenols form color compounds relevant in beer. Also see *polyphenol.*

terminal extract. The density of the fully fermented beer.

titration. Measurement of a substance in solution by the addition of a standard disclosing solution to initiate an indicative color change.

trisaccharide. A sugar composed of three monosaccharides joined by the removal of water molecules.

trub. Flocks of haze-forming particles resulting from the precipitation of proteins, hop oils, and tannins during boiling and cooling stages of brewing.

turbidity. Sediment in suspension; hazy, murky.

ullage. The empty space between a liquid and the top of its container. Also called airspace or headspace.

viscosity. The resistance of a fluid to flow.

volatile. Readily vaporized, especially esters, essential oils, and higher alcohols.

volume of beer. To calculate the approximate volumetric alcohol content, subtract the terminal gravity from the original gravity and divide the result by 75. For example: 1.050 − 1.012 = 0.038 / 0. 75 = .05 or 5% ABV.

water hardness. The degree of dissolved minerals in water. Usually expressed in parts per million (ppm) or grains per gallon (gpg).

wort. Mash extract (sweet wort); the hopped sugar solution before pitching, before it is fermented into beer.

Further Reading

Allen, Fal, and Jason Parker. "The Microbrewery Laboratory Manual—Part I: Yeast Management," *Brewing Techniques* 2, no. 4 (July/August 1994).

——. "The Microbrewery Laboratory Manual—Part II: Bacteria Detection, Enumeration, and Identification," *Brewing Techniques* 2, no. 5 (September/October 1994).

——. "The Microbrewery Laboratory Manual—Part III: Wild Yeast Detection and Remediation," *Brewing Techniques* 2, no. 6 (November/December 1994).

——. "The Microbrewery Laboratory Manual—Part IV: Advanced Laboratory Equipment," *Brewing Techniques* 3, no. 1 (January/February 1995).

Bachman, Tom. "Barley Wine—The King Kong of Beers," *Zymurgy* (Fall 1993).

Bibliography

Amsinck, G. S. *Practical Brewings: A Series of Fifty Brewings*. Lon
don: George Stewart Amsinck, 1868.

Fix, George. *Principles of Brewing Science*. Boulder, Colo.: Brewers
Publications, 1989.

Foster, Terry. *Pale Ale*. Boulder, Colo.: Brewers Publications, 1990.

Glover, Brian. *The Dictionary of Beer*. Hertfordshire: Campaign
for Real Ale.

Hanbury, Morris and Haas, John

Harrison, John, and the Durden Park Beer Club. *Old British Beers
and How to Make Them*.

Hough, J.S., D. E. Briggs, R. Stevens, and T. W. Young. *Malting
and Brewing Science*. Vols. 1 and 2. New York: Chapman
& Hall: 1982.

Huige, N. J. "Progress in Beer Oxidation Control," *Beer and Wine
Production*. B. H. Gump and D. J. Pruett, eds. Washington,
D.C.: American Chemical Society, 1993.

Jackson, Michael. *Michael Jackson's Beer Companion*. Philadelphia:
Running Press, 1993.

Lewis, Michael. *Stout*. Boulder, Colo.: Brewers Publications, 1995.

Master Brewer's Association of America. *The Practical Brewer*.
Madison, Wis.: MBAA, 1977.

Miller, Dave. *The Complete Handbook of Homebrewing*. Pownal,
Vt.: Storey Communications, 1988.

Noonan, Gregory. *New Brewing Lager Beer*. Boulder, Colo.: Brewers Publications, 1996.

———. *Scotch Ale*. Boulder, Colo.: Brewers Publications, 1993.

Priest, F. G., and I. Cambel. *Brewing Microbiology*. New York:
Chapman & Hall, 1996.

Rajotte, Pierre. *Belgian Ale*. Boulder, Colo.: Brewers Publications,
1992.

Wahl, Robert, and Henius, Max. *The American Handy Book of the
Brewing, Malting, and Auxiliary Trades*. 2 vols. Chicago:
Wahl-Henius Institute, 1908.

Index

AAUs. *See* Alpha acid units
Adambier, 29; data on, 125-26
Adjuncts, 58-59
Aeration, 68-69, 152
Aging, 73-75, 109; cellar temperature,
  110; cold, 73, 104-5, 154, 155;
  effects of, 43-44; hops and, 75;
  lengthy, 106, 108, 110; parameters
  for, 36-37; yeast and, 65
Alcohol, 31; parameters for, 32-34
Alcohol content, 3, 14, 109; taxation by,
  21-22
Alcohol tolerance, 67; yeast and, 65-66
Allen, A. F.: recipe by, 137
Alley Kat Brewing Co., 163
Alpha-amylase, 86
Alpha acids, 94
Alpha acid units (AAUs), 97
Altbier, 47
American Handy Book of Brewing, The
  (Wahl and Henius), 14
Amino acids, 91
Amsinc, G. S., 17
Anchor Brewing, 48; barley wine by,
  26-27
Anderson, Curt, 114
Appleton Brewing Co./Adler Brau, 157
Aroma, 54, 64, 98; finishing hops and, 97
Assets Grille/Southwest Brewing Co., 157
Atlantic Coast Brewing Ltd., 157
Attenuation, 86, 87; yeast and, 66-67
Autolysis, yeast, 104-5

Bacterias, 39, 44, 67; lactic acid, 76
Ballantine, 26

Bardo Rodeo, 157
Barleycorn, 36
Barley wine: American, 25-28, 63;
  British, 2, 6, 9, 42-44, 51, 63; dark,
  21; development of, 2, 4, 9-11, 13,
  16-25, 28-29, 41; families of, 42-52;
  marketing of, 22-23; mid-Atlantic,
  45 Northeastern U.S., 44-48; Northwestern U.S., 48-49; pale, 21, 95;
  permutations for, 22; studying, 6-7;
  technology for, 16-19
Barley Wine (Fix and Fix), recipe for,
  135-37
Barley Wine (Forhan), recipe for, 142-43
Barley wine-style ale, 3, 46
Barrel, 79
Bass: barley wine by, 23, 25; history of,
  20-21; labels for, 22; numbering sys-
  tem by, 20; water at, 70
Bass Museum Brewery, 51
Bass No. 1, 14, 15, 21, 24, 25, 48; data
  on, 112-13; paleness of, 42-43; start-
  ing gravity of, 33
Bass P2 Imperial Stout, 51
Bass, Ratcliff & Gretton, barley wine by,
  19-20
Batch 100: Barley Wine, recipe for, 133-34
Beach Chalet, The, 148
Beer Bellies, Inc., 148
Belgian Ale (Rajotte), 18
Belgian beers, 51
Bentley's, 16
Beowulf's Bark, data on, 116-17
Beta acid, 63
Beta-amylase, 86

B. Hwakker Brewing Co. Ltd., 163
Biberdorf, Clay, 120; recipe by, 132-33
Bicarbonate, avoiding, 71
Big beers, 9-11, 17, 37, 46, 48; American, 25; barley wine and, 11-16; brewing, 18, 26; British, 51; Germanic, 52; starting gravities of, 18; styles of, 50-51; tax restraints on, 45
Bigfoot, 27, 48-49, 147; cellaring, 110; data on, 114-15; malt for, 55
Big Time Brewing Co., 157
Bird Creek Brewery, 148
Birkebeiner Brewing Co., 157
Bitterness, 28, 30, 32, 62, 92, 96; astringent, 83; hop, 59, 60, 93-94; reducing, 95
Black Blaggart Barley Wine, recipe for, 137
Blending, 154
Blind Pig Brewing Co., 157
Bloomington Brewing Co./One World Enterprises, 157
Bluegrass Brewing Co., 157
Boardwalk Bistro, 158
Body, 58; yeast and, 38
Boiling, 60, 62, 90-91, 94, 95; closed system of, 93; evaporation and, 96-97; extra, 154; sweetness and, 56-57; turning/rolling of, 91, 92
Boston Beer Works, 158
Bottle conditioning, 40, 107-8; problems with, 155
Bottles, packaging in, 106-10
Brettanomyces, 39, 78
Breweries, barley wine, 111-29, 157-63
Brew house, 83-90
Brewing process, barley wine, 81-110
Brewsters Brewing Co. and Restaurant (No. 2), 163
Brewsters Brewing Co. and Restaurant/Cornerstone Inn (No. 3), 163
Brickskeller, 145, 147

BridgePort Brewing Co., 49, 158
Bright, 88
Brimstone Brewing Co., 158
Broad Ripple Brewing Co., 158
Brooklyn Brewing, imperial stout by, 51
Buffalo Bill's Barley Wine—Brown Sugar (How Come You Taste So Good?), recipe for, 138
Bureau of Alcohol, Tobacco, and Firearms, 3
Burton ales, 14, 15, 17, 26; starting gravities of, 16
Burton water, 71
Bush beer, 51
Butterfield Brewing Co., 158

Cafe on the Square and Brewpub, 158
Campaign for Real Ale (CAMRA): on barley wines, 41, 42; on winter beers, 42
Caramelization, 57, 91, 95
Carbonation, 69, 107; parameters for, 39-40
Carver Brewing Co., 158
Cascade hops, 63
Cascade Lakes Brewing Co., 158
Casks, lining, 78
Casting back, 100-101
Catherine the Great, ales for, 50
Cellaring, 109-10; temperature and, 108, 110
Centennial hops, 63
Challenger hops, 63
Champagne yeast, 38; alcohol tolerance of, 66
Charnick, Jeff, 129
Chilcot Charlie's, 149
Chinook hops, 60, 63
Chiswick Bitter, 43
Clarigen finings, 154
Clarity, 88; parameters for, 34-35

Cleanliness, concerns about, 44
Cloudiness, problems with, 154-55
Cohumulone, level of, 62
Coja, Maurice, 145-47
Colandria, internal/external, 91
Cold aging, 104-5, 154, 155; benefits of, 73
Color, 57, 58, 95; parameters for, 34-35
Columbus hops, 63
Conditioning: bottle, 40, 107-8, 155;
    cask, 40; long-term, 40; malt and,
    56; parameters for, 39-40
Cooling process, aeration during, 68-69
CooperSmith's Pub and Brewing, 158
Courage, 51
Crisp Malting, 1
Cusac's, 148, 149
Cyclops (Old One Eye), data on, 126-27

Daniels, Ray: recipe by, 133-34
DE. See Diatomaceous earth
De Dolle Brouwers, 51
De Hemel brewery, 52
Denali Brewery, 148
Diacetyl, reducing, 73, 104
Diatomaceous earth (DE), 106
Dictionary of Beer (Glover), 41
Dock Street Brewery and Restaurant
    (No. 2), 158
Dock Street Brewing Co. Brewery and
    Restaurant, 158
Donnelly, Sean, 116
Drinkability, 109
Dry hopping, 6, 98
Dubuisson brewery, 51
Durden Park Beer Club, research/experi-
    mentation by, 15

East Kent hops, 63
Eckhardt, Fred: recipe by, 139-40
Effervescence, 40
Eisbock, 52

EKU 28, 52
Eldridge Pope brewery, Thomas Hardy
    Ale by, 23-24
El Toro Brewing Co., 158
Elysian Brewing Co., 158
Enzymes, 86, 105
Equipment, 31, 90, 91; British, 47
Eske's Brew Pub/Sangre de Cristo Brew-
    ing Co., 158
Esters, 43, 102; yeast and, 38, 64-65
Eugene City Brewing Co./West Brothers
    Bar B-Q, 158
Evaporation: original gravity and, 95;
    rate of, 96-97
Exchange Brewery, 24
Extract fortification, 6

Fahrendorf, Terri, 116
Faultline Brewing Co. Inc., 158
Fermentables, 55, 58
Fermentation, 67, 92, 99, 155; check-
    ing, 2; cold, 39; completion of,
    103-4; cylindroconical, 100, 105; of
    high gravity beers, 101-4; problems
    with, 100, 150-51; temperature of,
    101, 102-3; yeast and, 66, 103
Fermenters, 151; closed, 150; copper,
    102, 102 (photo)
Festivals, 145-49
Filtration, 73, 105-6, 155; flavor and, 105
Finishing gravities, 16, 36, 59, 103
Finishing hops, 30, 32, 62-63, 97-98;
    aroma/flavor and, 97
Firestone, fermentation vessels at, 78
Fish Brewing Co./Fishbowl Pub, 159
Fix, George: on dark malts, 37; recipe
    by, 135-37
Fix, Laurie: recipe by, 135-37
Flat Branch Brewing Co., 159
Flavor, 59, 60; discussing, 53-54; filtra-
    tion and, 105; finished, 28; hop, 93,

97; malt, 54, 57; temperature and, 110; yeast and, 37-38, 64-65

Flocculation, 92; yeast and, 67-68

Flying Dog Brewpub, 159

Forhan, Kevin: recipe by, 142-43

Free Mash Tun Act (1880), 32

French oak, 78-79

Fructose, 66

Fuggle hops, 63

Fuller's, 18, 24, 43

Full Sail Brewpub and Tasting Room, 159

Fur Rondez-vous, 149

GABF. *See* Great American Beer Festival

Gale's Brewery, 24, 33, 46-47; conditioning at, 78

Galena hops, 62

Glacier Brewhouse, 148, 149

Glacier Brewhouse Barley Wine, data on, 128-29

Glatt Bros. Brewing Co., 163

Glover, Brian: on barley wine, 41

Glucose, 66

Golden City Brewery, 159

Golden Pride, 24, 43; data on, 115-16

Golding hops, 63

Gold Label, 21, 22, 24, 34, 41

Goose Island Brewing Co., 159; aging at, 79

Grade, 106

Grant, Bert: imperial stout by, 51

Gravities, 31, 109; reading, 154. *See also* Finishing gravities; Starting gravities

Great Alaskan Winter Brew and Barley Wine Festival, 148-49

Great American Beer Festival (GABF), barley wine and, 27, 41, 50

Great Dane Pub and Brewing Co., 159

Grizzly Bay Brewing Co., 159

"Guidelines to Beer Styles and Medal Categories" (GABF), 41

Guinness Book of Records, on Hardy Ale, 24

Gypsum, adding, 95

Hair of the Dog Brewing, parti-gyle and, 29

Hall, Greg: aging by, 79

Hampshire Brewery, 77 (photo)

Hansell, John: on packaged beer, 75-76

Hart Brewing Co. Inc., 159

Hartman, Mike, 119

Harvard Brewery, refectory brewery at, 25

Harvest Ale, 33

Haze, removing, 105

Hemocytometer, 99, 100

High-gravity beers, 10, 14, 28, 60; aging, 73, 74-75; bottle conditioning of, 107; fermentation of, 101-4; overpitching/ underpitching, 99-100; water for, 70; yeast and, 38

Hop chart, 61

Hoppiness, 28, 59

Hopping rates, 60, 109

Hops, 50, 53, 59-63; alpha acid contents of, 62; aroma, 36; bitterness of, 59, 60, 93-94; boiling, 60, 62; British, 63; choosing, 60; cultivation of, 19; flavor of, 59, 93; German, 63; Northwestern U.S., 49; parameters for, 35-36; pellet, 98; problems with, 153-54. *See also* Finishing hops

Hops Bistro and Brewery (No. 1), 159

Horndean, 33, 46-47

Hot break, 92

Hubcap Brewery and Kitchen, 159

Humboldt Brewery, 159

Humes Brewing Co. Inc., 159

Humpy's, 148, 149

Humulinic, 94

Hürlimann's, 52

Hydrometers, 9

IBU. *See* International bitterness units
Imperial stout, 20, 50, 51; aging, 79
India pale ale, American brewing of, 27
Ingredients, considering, 31
Innovation, experimentation and, 131
International bitterness units (IBU), 59, 97
Iron, 71, 73
Isinglass, 154
Iso-alpha-acids, 60, 93, 94
Isomerization, 91, 94

Jackson, Michael, 50
Jim Beam barrels, aging in, 79
Joe's Brewing Co., 159

Kalamazoo Brewing Company, 45
Keene, David, 146 (photo); barley wine
     festival and, 147-48
Kegs, packaging in, 106-10
Kettles, 96
Kipling, Rudyard S., 113
Knocking out, 69, 100-101
Kulmbach, 52
Kulmbacher Reichelbräu, 52

Lactic acid, 14, 17, 76
Lactobacillus, 39, 76
Lafayette Brewing Co., 159
Lautering, 90
Lauter tun, 18, 83-84, 152
Lee, ale by, 33
Lewis, Michael: on imperial stout, 50
Liberty hops, 63
London Pride, 43
Lucky 13, 148
Lupulin, 48

MacDonald, Maurice: Beer Bellies and,
     148
McGuire's Irish Pub and Brewery, 160
McNeill's Brewery, 160

Mad River Brewing Co., 159
Magnum hops, 62
Maier, John: imperial stout by, 51
Malt Advocate (Hansell), 75-76
Malt bill, 54-59, 109
Malting, floor, 55
Malt liquors, 3, 12
Maltose, 66
Maltotetraose, 67
Maltotriose, 66
Malts: British, 55; choosing, 54, 57-58;
     crystal, 57-58; dextrin, 58; flavor of,
     54, 58; Munich, 58; pale, 17, 54-56;
     58; Scottish distiller's, 1; six-row, 55;
     specialty, 56-58; two-row, 55; under-
     modified, 84
Malt syrups, qualities of, 34
Malt wines, 12
Malzwein Alt Barley Wine ("German
     Experiment"), recipe for, 134-35
Manchester, 33
Marin Brewing Co., 160
Marris Otter pale malt, 1, 55
Marstons, fermentation vessels at, 78
Martinez, Charles, 117
Mash, 82; consistency of, 86; setting,
     84; temperature of, 87
Mash bed, 84; compacting, 82, 89;
     problems with, 89, 151-53
Mash tun, 18, 83-84, 85 (photo), 89;
     overfilling, 85-86
Melanoidins, 57, 95
Metal "stone," 69
Methylene blue staining test, 99
Microbreweries, barley wine and, 10,
     26-27
Microflora/microorganisms, problems
     with, 44, 76, 155
Midnight Sun Brewery, 148
Milling, 82-83
Minerals, maximum levels of, 70

Mishawaka Brewing Co., 160
Moline, Rob: recipe by, 143-44
Monster (1996), data on, 118-19
Monster mash, 84-87
Mosher, Randy: recipe by, 141-42
Murphys Creek Brewing Co., 160
My Old Flame Barley Wine, recipe for, 141-42

Napa ABValley Brewing Co., 160
New Brewing Lager Beer (Noonan), 63
Noonan, Gregory: on caramelized wort sugars, 57; recipe by, 140-41; on yeast, 63-64
Northdown hops, 63
Northern Brewer hops, 62
Numbering system, 20-21

Oak, 79
Oats, adding, 35
O'Brady's, 148, 149
Old ales, 13, 14, 46, 47
Old Bawdy Barley Wine (1994), 2, 5, 28; data on, 121-22
Old British Beers and How to Make Them (Durden Park Beer Club), 16
Old Crustacean, 28
Old Dominion Brewing Co., 160
Old Foghorn (1996), 26, 48; data on, 120-21
Old Gander, data on, 119-20
Old Headcracker, 33
Old Knucklehead, 49
Old Nick, 24
Old Possum, data on, 118
Old Weasel, data on, 114
Oliver, Garrett, 118; imperial stout by, 51
Opinsky, Bill: Beer Bellies and, 148
Oregon Adambier—A Barley Wine-style Ale, recipe for, 139-40
Organic material, avoiding, 71

Ottolini, James, 118
Overpitching, 99-100
Owens, Bill: recipe by, 138
Oxygen, 109; packaged beers and, 107; yeast and, 68-69

Pacific Coast Brewing Co., 160
Pacific Hop Exchange, 160
Packaging, 36-37, 75-76; options for, 106-10; oxygen and, 107; problems with, 44
Papazian, Charlie: recipe by, 134-35
Particulates, avoiding, 71
Parti-gyle, 4, 18, 25, 29, 43
Pellet hops, 98
pH: kettle, 94-95; wort, 94-95
Phenolic substances, 92
Pike Brewing Company, 28, 160; aging, 79; yeast for, 65
Pike Place Brewery, barley wine by, 1, 2, 5
Pitching rate, 99-100
Pizza Port/Solana Beach Brewery, 160
Practical Brewings: A Series of Fifty Brewings (Amsinck), 17
Pre-boiling, 73
Prescott Brewing Co., 160
Priming, 40, 108
Principles of Brewing Science (Fix), 37
Prize Old Ale, 24, 33, 47; conditioning of, 78; data on, 127-28
Proteins, 91; haze-forming, 105
Pyramid Anniversary Ale (1995), data on, 120

Quality Assured Brewing, 160

Railway Brewing Company, 149
Rail Yard Brewery, 148
Rajotte, Pierre, 18
Recipes, barley wine, 131-44
Recirculation, 87-88

Rest, warm, 104
Richbrau Brewing Co., 160
Rio Bravo Restaurant & Brewery, 160
Road House, data on, 117
Rob's "Big 12" Barley Wine, recipe for, 143-44
Rock Bottom Brewery (No. 2), 160
Rogue Ales/Oregon Brewing Co., 161
Rogue Brewing, 28; imperial stout by, 51
Roller mills, 82
Rousing, 67, 103, 151
Rubicon Brewing Co., 161
Rudyard's Rare, data on, 113
Runoff, 88-90, 152, 153

Saccharomyces, 17, 64
St. Stan's Brewery/Pub and Restaurant, 161
Saint Louis Brewery/Schlafly Brands, 161
Samichlaus, 52
Samuel Smith's, 51
San Francisco Brewing Co., 161
Santa Cruz Brewing Co. and Front Street Pub, 161
Santa Fe Brewing Co., 161
Santa Rosa Brewing Co., 161
Schenk HS 6000/AF 6000, 106
Scotch ale, sweetness of, 57
Scotch Ale (Noonan), 57
Seabright Brewery Inc., 161
Seattle Brewers, 161
Shaftebury Brewing Co. Ltd., 163
Shipyard Brewing Co., 161
Sierra Nevada Brewing Co., 48-49, 161; barley wine by, 27; malt for, 55
Sleeping Lady Brewery, 148
Sleepwalker Barley Wine, recipe for, 140-41
Small beer, 29, 90, 153
Smell, problems with, 156
Smith, Hubert, 124
Snow Goose Brewery, 149

Sonoma Brewing Co., 161
Southern Oregon and Pacific Brewing Company Brewing Company Barley Wine, data on, 124-25
Spanish Peaks Brewery, 161
Spanish Peaks Brewing Co., 161
Sparge, 18, 88-90
Special Old Ale, data on, 129
Specialty malts, choosing, 56-58
Spice, adding, 35
Spoilage, concern about, 12
Stabilization, 91-93
Stack condensers, 93
Starting gravities, 2-3, 14, 17, 32, 33-34, 36, 49, 51, 67; big beer, 18; elevated, 4, 12; evaporation and, 95; taxation by, 21-22
Stille Nacht, 51
Stock ale, 13, 14-15
Stout (Lewis), 50
Straining, 90, 98
Strong ales, 13, 14, 15, 17, 19, 50; American, 26
Style, proper versions of, 31
Sucrose, 66
Sugars, 36, 55, 66, 67, 85, 88, 90; caramelized, 57; excess, 34; fermentable/unfermentable, 91; non-malt, 58; qualities of, 34
Sunday River Brewing Co., 161
Suspension, 103, 108, 150
Sutter Brewing Co. Inc., 162
Sweetness, 58, 59; boiling and, 56-57; unfermentables and, 87
Syrups, 36; qualities of, 34

Taxation, 21-22, 45
Temperature, 9; cellaring, 109, 110; fermentation, 64, 69; flavor and, 110
Tennent's, 22, 24, 34; pale barley wine by, 21

Thames, 42-44
Thinness, 39
Third Coast Old Ale, 45
Thomas Hardy Ale, 23-24, 52; data on, 122-24
Thomas Hardy Brewery, alcoholic fruit drinks by, 24
Tomson and Wotton, 16
Toronado's, barley wine festival by, 147-48
Traffic Jam and Snug, 162
Trent, 42-44
Trinity Beer Works Inc., 162
Troy Brewing Co., 162
Truman XXK March Keeping Ale (1832), 16
Tsampa Barley Wine, recipe for, 132-33
Twenty Tank Brewery, 148, 162
TwoRows Restaurant and Brewery, 162

Umpqua Brewing Co., 162
Underpitching, 99-100
Unfermentables, 86, 91; sweetness and, 87
Unit conversion chart, 164

Vorlauf, 87-88

Walnut Brewery, 162
Water: impact of, 69-71, 73; maximum levels of minerals in, 70; pre-boiling, 73
Weinkeller Brewpub (No. 2), 162
Wendling, Shawn, 128

Wheat, adding, 35
Wheat wines, 35
Whitbread, 24, 41
Wild Duck Brewery and Restaurant, 162
Wild River Brewing and Pizza Co. (No. 2), 162
Winter ales, 5
Winter Warmer, 46
Wood, aging on, 76, 78-79
Wort, 87, 89; aerating, 152; boiling, 91, 92, 95; concentration of, 96; cooling, 100-101; diluting, 152; drawing off, 98; evaporation of, 93; gravity of, 94; hopped, 97-98; infection of, 101
Worthington Burton ale, 14
Wyeast, 64
Wynkoop Brewing Co., 162

Yakima Brewing and Malting, imperial stout by, 51
Yeast, 19, 39, 53, 63-69; alcohol tolerance and, 65-66; American, 68; attenuation and, 66-67; autolysis of, 104-5; British, 68; champagne, 38, 66; fermentation and, 66, 103; flavor of, 64-65; flocculation and, 67-68; healthy, 99; lager, 38; liquid, 99; oxygen and, 68-69; parameters for, 37-39; pitching, 98-99
Young, 24

Zeitgeist Motorcycle Club, 148
Zimmermann, Steve: recipe by, 143-44

About the Authors

Fal Allen grew up in Hilo, a small town on the island of Hawaii. He graduated from the University of Hawaii in 1984 and moved to the Northwest that same year.

Fal had an inordinately large interest in beer starting at an early age. This fascination continued through college and led to further investigations into the realm of beer styles and brewing. He started homebrewing in 1985 and has been a professional brewer since 1988. He has held his current position as head brewer for the Pike Brewing Company in Seattle, Washington, for the last eight years.

Fal has authored many articles about beer and brewing but is most proud of the five-part series on microbiology and laboratory procedures that appeared in *Brewing Techniques* and of his collaborative effort with Dick Cantwell and Kevin Forhan on how to produce cask-conditioned beer in America. Fal currently writes a regular column in *American Brewer* under the title "I, Beer Thrall."

Although it doesn't seem like it at times, Fal does have a life outside brewing. He also enjoys camping, ocean activities, gardening, motor bikes, and traveling (hopefully to somewhere that has good beer).

Dick Cantwell was born in Germany and raised in Wisconsin and Minnesota. He has lived all over the place, including Chicago, New York, Philadelphia, Los Angeles, Madrid, Boston, Michigan, and western Montana. He has lived in Seattle for the past eight years, where his professional brewing career began as head brewer at Duwamps Cafe/Seattle Brewing Company. Since then, he has worked at Pike Place Brewery and served as head brewer at Big Time Brewery. With partners David Buhler and Joe Bisacca, he began Elysian Brewing Company and Public House in 1996. In addition to brewing, Dick has written two novels and various stories and plays. These days his writing mainly has to do with beer, in the pages of various magazines, including a regular column in *American Brewer*. He has two frequently wonderful children, Lucy and Nap.